KEEPING REPTILES AND AMPHIBIANS

KEEPING REPTILES AND AMPHIBIANS

ALFRED LEUTSCHER

CHARLES SCRIBNER'S SONS

New York

Printed in Great Britain
Library of Congress Catalog Card Number 75–46103
ISBN 0–684–14656–8

Contents

List of Illustrations

8

Introduction:
The Approach to Reptiles

A confession to a real love for amphibians and reptiles usually draws amused comments from tolerant friends and relatives, but to reveal that one actually keeps such animals as crocodiles, snakes, toads and salamanders is, they may say, going a bit too far.

The keeping and study of amphibians and reptiles, called herpetology (Greek, herpeton = a crawling thing) is becoming increasingly popular. Once the reluctance, dislike, fear and even hatred of these much misunderstood and mostly harmless animals is overcome by closer acquaintance, the owner will soon become engrossed in a particularly fascinating pursuit. To many people the first experience of handling a 'slimy snake' comes as relief and revelation. As for the 'lounge lizard', just try and catch one!

This centuries-old antipathy towards reptiles and amphibians is hard to explain. Could it be an instinctive fear we are born with? Does it stem from some tradition, is religion involved, or is it just downright ignorance and bad instruction? Probably a bit of each. In an odd kind of way it is we, the Western peoples, who treat, or rather abuse, these animals, by perpetuating the quaint and often erroneous beliefs which make up so much of our folklore and legend. In more primitive societies the approach is more direct, if misguided, for here the animals, in particular the snake, are venerated and given a better status than that of the mere 'snake in the grass'. For the early Christians the snake was the Devil's disciple, yet in India the cobra is sacred to the

Hindu. The early Greeks symbolised their god of healing in the person of a serpent.

If we can excuse the ignorant and superstitious layman, we might expect a more tolerant attitude from the scholar. Yet this has not always been the case, and amphibians and reptiles got away to a bad start. At the height of the era of eighteenth-century learning an upsurge of collecting, studying and classifying plants and animals was inspired by the Swedish botanist Carl von Linné (Linnaeus), with the publication of his famous work, the *Systema Natura*. Unfortunately he was not a herpetologist, and he had no great regard for these animals, as can be seen from his description of a somewhat mixed-up group which he called Classis Amphibia:

> These foul and loathsome animals are distinguished by a heart with a single ventricle and a single auricle, doubtful lungs and a double penis. Most amphibia are abhorrent because of their cold bodies, pale colour, cartilaginous skeletons, filthy skin, fierce aspect, calculating eye, offensive smell, harsh voice, squalid habitation, and terrible venom; and so their Creator has not exerted his powers to create many of them.

Small wonder that many a promising naturalist breathed an Amen, and went over to another group!

Today the situation is changed. The growing band of enthusiasts, young and adult, amateur and professional, who are taking up the pursuit of herpetology, either as a hobby or as a profession, are making new discoveries about these animals' habits and life-histories, so different from our own. And there is still much to learn.

The species chosen for this book are those most likely to come the way of the herpetologist pet-keeper, either by discovery or through the trade. Venomous species are deliberately omitted, partly because of the risk of a bite, and partly because they tend to be temperamental and difficult to feed in captivity. Should a venomous snake be kept, never take liberties. Sooner or later most herpetologists receive a bite, either through carelessness or over-confidence. As the author knows from experience, the result is by no means pleasant.

10

Every newcomer to the hobby of herpetology should bear two things in mind. Firstly, amphibians, either through being abused or killed on sight, or from being over-collected, are becoming rare. Others are fast losing their natural habitats. No rare specimen should be collected, or bought from a dealer, since the possession of a rarity is contrary to today's urgent need for conservation and protection of our diminishing wildlife. Secondly, since an animal in captivity is at the mercy of its owner, it should be given every proper care for its well-being. A sickly animal is a poor advertisement for its keeper, and can bring the hobby of herpetology into disrepute.

It is hoped that this book, intended for the pet-keeper and naturalist, will be a useful source of information, as well as a guide to the care and understanding of an especially interesting group of animals.

CHAPTER 1

Vivarium Construction

THE vivarium hobby, as the keeping of amphibians and reptiles is usually called, first became popular in Victorian times. Originally the word (Latin, vivus = living) had a wide application, and referred to such different things as a place for live game, a warren for rabbits, even a fish-pond. Today it is restricted more to an artificial domicile, such as a cage or glass tank containing suitable plants and soil, for amphibians or reptiles. The pond or reptiliary provides outdoor accommodation. In the Victorian conservatory or fernery the ideal conditions were created for the housing of many kinds of plants, exotic as well as native. This later became modified into an ornamental plant cage, or vivarie. Then, with more emphasis placed on the animal contents, the vivarium hobby was on its way.

As a home for reptiles or amphibians, a vivarium can take many forms and sizes, depending upon the numbers and kinds of specimens kept, and to some extent on the owner's pocket and workmanship. Since amphibians and reptiles live in a wide range of habitats, from purely aquatic to dry desert, and from the warm Tropics to countries with cold winters, a number of vivaria have been selected, in order to provide one or other of the six basic requirements—wet or dry surroundings, sunshine or shade, and a temperate or warm atmosphere. These requirements will also apply to the plants which are used, thus some knowledge of plants and their needs would help in planning the contents of the vivarium in which the animals will spend their days. A plant list is provided on page 153.

The Glass Vivarium (Fig 1)

The simplest and most readily made indoor vivarium is a large glass bowl, an accumulator tank, or a converted fish-aquarium. These have the advantage of being watertight, and also allow an unrestricted view of the occupants. A cover may not be necessary, so long as the sides are steep enough to prevent escapes; however it will be necessary with tree-frogs, geckos and small amphibians whose feet can cling to glass.

1A *The 'wet' vivarium for amphibians*

When in the land stage most amphibians choose damp and shady surroundings. A good depth of loamy soil, into which

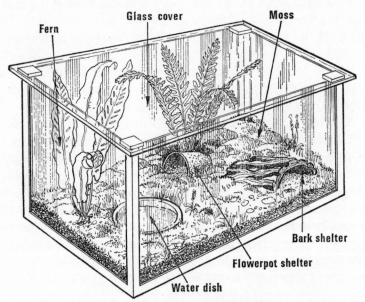

Fig 1A 'Wet' vivarium for amphibians

some amphibians like to burrow, should cover the floor space. Hiding places can be provided by using pieces of curved bark, brickwork, or flowerpots split into two, lengthwise and placed

14

on their sides. Shade and moisture-loving plants can be planted in between, or sunk in their pots if there is room. Various mosses and small ferns, also houseplants which enjoy a damp and shady atmosphere, can be used. Leave a space for a shallow dish of water sunk to its rim in the soil.

Cover this vivarium with a sheet of glass, resting on corner supports of rubber or cork, leaving the aperture narrow enough to prevent escapes. This will help to retain the humidity as the water evaporates from the dish, and transpires from the plants. Keep the dish regularly topped up with fresh, clean water, preferably rain-water. A water spray is a useful accessory for giving the contents an occasional damping. A slight disadvantage is the condensation on the glass, which obscures the view. This can be partly avoided by using a cover which is half glass and half-perforated zinc. Fitted into a frame this can be attached to the aquarium top, and removed when necessary.

Such a vivarium would suit a number of frogs, toads and land salamanders. It should be placed in a shady corner, away from sunshine, in cool surroundings unless the inmates happen to be tropical.

1B *The 'dry' vivarium for reptiles*
Most reptiles prefer dry surroundings. Using a similar glass container, cover the floor with a mixture of dry earth and sand or peat, and sink a water-dish which will be used only for drinking purposes. A small drinking dish is all that is required, but it must be firmly fixed so that it cannot be upset or spilled. As in the 'wet' vivarium, bark, broken flowerpots and brickwork can be used for shelter. Plants adapted to dry conditions, such as cacti, succulents and houseplants used to bright but dry surroundings, can be planted.

It is important that lizards and snakes should have something to rub against when about to shed their old skins. Loose clumps of dry moss, bracken or heather could be used, as well as a branch or two through which the animals can crawl.

A common error in keeping lizards or snakes is to allow the vivarium to become too wet by over-watering the plants. A

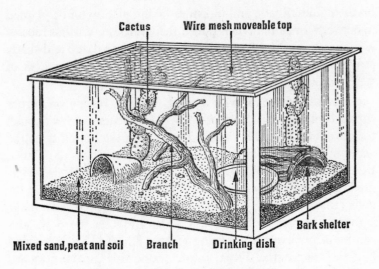

Fig 1B 'Dry' vivarium for reptiles

constantly wet reptile specimen may have difficulty in sloughing, and this can lead to bacterial or fungal infection, a danger to health. So although a well-arranged vivarium containing plants and soil gives a more natural aspect, and seems desirable, there are snags. In the confined space the inmates may disturb the plants by their movements and possible digging habits. The plants themselves give off moisture which can upset the desired dry atmosphere. Soil may harbour mites—a bare floor makes for easier cleaning (healthy animals usually excrete solid, chalky droppings which can be readily removed or mopped up.) For these reasons, some herpetologists prefer their snakes and lizards to live in bare and austere surroundings.

Openings, such as a frame of perforated zinc, are best situated at the top of the vivarium. Openings placed on top minimise the risk of escapes with lively specimens. Avoid using wire netting as they may rub their noses raw on this.

The Metal Vivarium (Fig 2)
This type of vivarium can be home-made or purchased from the trade. It usually consists of tin sheeting fixed to a metal frame.

16

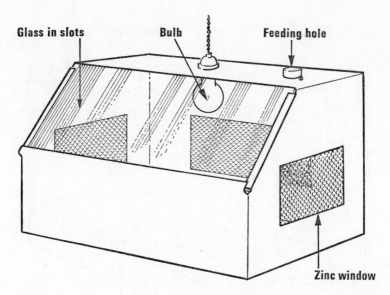

Glass in slots   Bulb   Feeding hole

Zinc window

Fig 2   Metal vivarium

The design shown, made by the author, was used for a number of years, housing a succession of lizards and snakes. The dimensions were approximately 2ft long × 1ft deep and 1ft tall at the back, sloping down to 6in at the front. An angle-iron frame had tin sheeting welded on to the bottom, rear, sides and front. Squares cut out of the sides and back were covered with perforated zinc for ventilation. A hole cut into the top held a socket for a light-bulb. A sheet of removable glass fitted into slots along the sloping top. This was held in position by a stay-bar in front, and secured with swivel catches at the back. All the metalwork was painted with a waterproof coat, white inside and green outside.

Metal has the advantage of being stronger and more durable than woodwork. The formation of rust, usually due to neglect, is the only disadvantage. Some authorities feel that contact with metal can be injurious, but this has not been my experience.

The Wooden Vivarium (Fig 3)
When making a vivarium from wood, you have unlimited

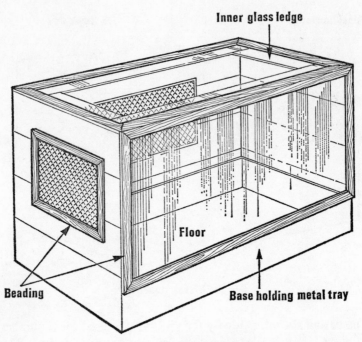

Inner glass ledge

Floor

Beading

Base holding metal tray

Fig 3 Wooden vivarium

scope in its design and finish. Apart from its main purpose of
housing the animals, it can be made aesthetically pleasing to
the eye, and used as an additional piece of furniture.

The example shown was made by the author, stood in the
hallway for a number of years, and housed a succession of
salamanders, frogs and toads. It was 3ft long × 18in tall × 1ft
deep. The base was made of ⅜in planking (planed dealwood),
3in deep, and contained a metal tray. Sides and back of similar
wood rose from this base, joined at the corners with ¾in square
uprights. Windows of perforated zinc were let into these. The
front glass was slotted into upright grooves, and could be taken
out when required. To give a picture effect the glass and the
zinc windows were framed with beading.

This vivarium had an open top, but, to discourage escapes,
had a rim along the inner edge made of strips of glass 3in wide.

18

On the occasion when a chameleon was kept, the top was covered with a perforated zinc frame. A door can of course be fitted in the roof if preferred.

The metal tray was filled with a loamy soil, and contained the usual hiding places, water-dish and plants. The inside was painted with a white waterproof paint, and the outside stained dark oak to match the surrounding furniture. The time, labour and modest expense involved were amply matched by the pleasure and instruction which this 'eye-catching' vivarium gave to the family, and to guests.

With a little searching it is possible to unearth a ready-made wooden vivarium at a sale or a junk shop. Occasionally one can pick up an old showcase used in displaying wares, and this makes an excellent home. All it may require is a small modification to let in some air; and to see that it does not leak, if soil and plants are to be incorporated.

The Tropical Vivarium (Fig 4)

Apart from what has already been recommended for the contents of the vivarium, whether wet or dry, some heating may be required for species of tropical origin. A simple method is to suspend a light-bulb which will give off radiant heat as well as light. This warmth can be intensified by fitting the bulb socket into the lid of a tin so that the bulb, when inserted, is enclosed. This arrangement gives off a surprising amount of heat. Alternatively, an infra-red tube can be used; there are a number of models on the market. Since heat rises, such devices should be placed near the bottom of the vivarium. Wherever a heat source is placed it should always be covered in some way with netting, so as to protect the occupants; some reptiles will actually rest against a heat source, and suffer burns. Better still, fit the vivarium with a false bottom of strong, fine-mesh wire netting or perforated zinc, with the heat source beneath. Heat will then rise to warm the soil and the air above.

Needless to say, if constant heat, such as a radiator, is available, the vivarium could be placed above this, if there is room.

19

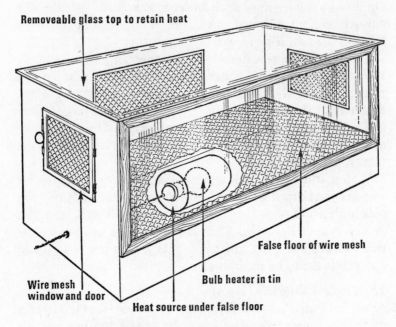

Removeable glass top to retain heat

False floor of wire mesh

Bulb heater in tin

Wire mesh
window and door

Heat source under false floor

Fig 4   Tropical vivarium

The Aquarium (Fig 5)

Used as a water container for aquatic species, the fish-aquarium is ready-made for this purpose. It is very suitable for those amphibians which are aquatic, or which breed in water, as well as for terrapins and small specimens of crocodilians.

First, inspect the tank for leakages, and thoroughly clean out with soapy water, adding some disinfectant, so as to kill off any impurities. The aquarium sand available from dealers is a good planting medium. The particles are of the right size for the roots of water plants to gain a hold. Finer material such as sea-sand is not advised, as it tends to become impacted, and is not so easy to free from pollution. The aquarium sand should slope from back to front so that any accumulating organic debris, the so-called detritus, will tend to drift towards the front. It can then be more easily siphoned away. A certain

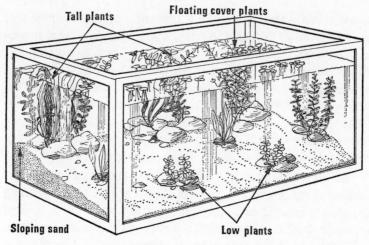

Tall plants Floating cover plants

Sloping sand Low plants

Fig 5 Aquarium

amount should be left, as this is a valuable food material for the plants.

Before adding water, place the selection of plants in position. They can be anchored in the sand with small stones. Tall plants should go to the sides and rear, small ones in front, and the more bushy kinds in the centre. Natural stone can also be added. One should aim at building up a rising landscape, arranging the rocks in steps, after the fashion of a rock garden. Plants can then be placed in the pockets between the rocks. A visit to an aquarium show, where there is usually a 'furnished aquaria' contest, will show what attractive displays can be created.

Plants provide a three-fold benefit. They give decoration, supply oxygen, and provide a spawning medium, especially for some amphibians such as newts. Floating plants act as a screen against too much light, and give cover to young and small specimens.

Fill the tank, if possible, with rain or pond water. If tap-water is used, allow it to stand for a few days outdoors. The water should be poured into a saucer laid on the bottom, so as to

21

disturb the plants as little as possible. Now leave for a few days, to allow the water to mature. At first it may turn cloudy, due to the spread of bacteria. A green colour indicates that microscopic plants, called algae, are appearing. Then, as microscopic animals appear to feed on this, the water clears. In this matured condition it takes on an indefinable 'bloom', and, so long as the balance is maintained, will remain like this indefinitely. To hasten the water-clearing process some aquarium owners introduce members of the water-flea family which feed on algae, or a freshwater mussel which filters algae from the water.

The tank is now ready for occupants such as newts, water salamanders, possibly a pair of frogs or toads in breeding condition. Having bred they may require removal to a land vivarium, but the offspring will remain until they metamorphose.

Healthy, matured water has a peculiar but not unpleasant smell to it. Any objectionable odour of pollution should immediately be investigated. It could be an overlooked dead animal, or decaying food. Remove the cause, half empty the tank, and top up. If things have gone too far, then remove the occupants, empty the tank, and start again. Some evaporation of water will always take place, so topping-up is necessary. A cover of glass on corner supports will limit this loss of water, and also prevent escapes.

Apart from possible pollution, there is another nuisance, in itself a healthy sign, caused by excessive light: the plants grow too fast and crowd the tank, and will need thinning. Some extra screening may be required.

The idea that an air-pump is necessary to maintain oxygen is a fallacy. Oxygen will always dissolve into the water, until saturation is reached. The value of a pump is in the rising air-bubbles which help to circulate the water. This brings undesirable gases such as carbon dioxide to the surface, where they can more readily disperse into the atmosphere.

The Aqua-terrarium (Fig 6)
Most amphibians spend part of their lives on land, and part in water. They either grow up in water, or go there to breed. To

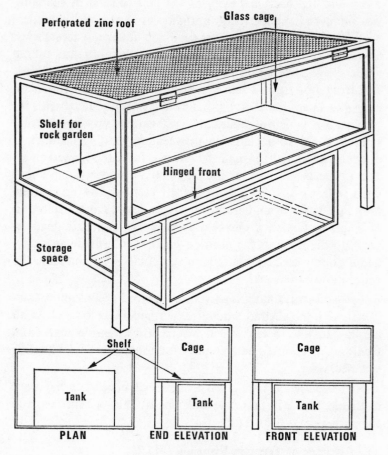

Perforated zinc roof
Glass cage
Shelf for rock garden
Hinged front
Storage space
Shelf
Cage
Cage
Tank
Tank
Tank
PLAN
END ELEVATION
FRONT ELEVATION

Fig 6   Aqua-terrarium

obviate the necessity of transferring them from a land vivarium to an aquarium, and vice-versa, the two habitats can be combined.

The author's attempt at making an aqua-terrarium worked well for many years, and there were a number of breeding successes with newts, and with some species of frogs and toads. The illustration shows that it consisted of a kind of glass-house erected over and around a specially made aquarium. This stood on a wooden stand against the wall of a sunroom.

Around the back and sides of the tank a shelf of planking was fitted and supported on uprights, as shown. Space underneath could be used for storing food and aquarium accessories, concealed from view by a curtain. Above the tank, and taking in the shelves, was a cage of glass with a roof of perforated zinc. The front was framed like a window, and could be raised on hinges to open like a skylight. The shelving was lined with tin sheeting on which a miniature rock garden was built, using suitable rocks with plants in between. A winding channel of cement meandered through the garden, from the highest point to a low rock jutting over the tank rim. A hidden pump circulated water so that it was in constant motion, flowing into the tank in a series of miniature waterfalls. Apart from a selection of small rock plants, climbers such as ivy and philodendron grew up the sides of the glass cage. The tank, made specially, had a sloping end, so that the inmates could enter and leave the water more easily.

This somewhat ambitious venture proved a constant attraction and interest, and housed a permanent colony of small amphibians and reptiles which needed little attention apart from feeding. All were temperate species so that no artificial heating was necessary.

No measurements are given, as these will depend on the space available. In this instance the tank was 4ft long × 18in deep, and the glass cage was 3ft tall.

The Alligator or Terrapin Vivarium (Fig 7)
Those reptiles which are carnivorous by nature, and spend part of their lives in water, are best kept to themselves. This applies to most terrapins, as well as to alligators and crocodiles. Depending upon their size (only young specimens are usually kept), an aquarium is quite adequate. It is divided down the centre, lengthwise, by a wall of bricks, or a piece of log cut to size. One side is filled with aquarium sand, to a depth of about 6in. Heating can be supplied by sinking an aquarium heater into the sand. Water in the other half, to a depth of about 4in, will seep through the sand. Warmth from the heater will pass

24

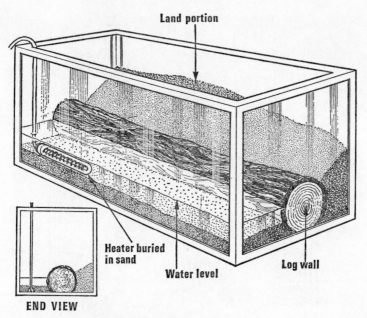

Land portion

Heater buried
in sand

Water level

Log wall

END VIEW

Fig 7   Alligator or terrapin vivarium

from sand to water, and also warm the air above. If necessary a
glass cover can be used to hold in the heat.

The tank can be placed over a radiator to receive heat, or on
a metal base with a spirit-lamp beneath.

The Tree-Frog and Chameleon Cage (Fig 8)
This is merely a modification of the wooden vivarium, which is
tall enough to take pot-plants, climbers and a few branches.
The plants can simply be inserted in their pots, and the spaces
between packed with loamy soil or moss. Its purpose is to house
such species as certain snakes and lizards which climb, also
anoles, chameleons and tree-frogs. Here again, the kind of
showcase seen in shops would be ideal.

Other Indoor Enclosures
In the more sophisticated fish-aquarium hobby, which has a

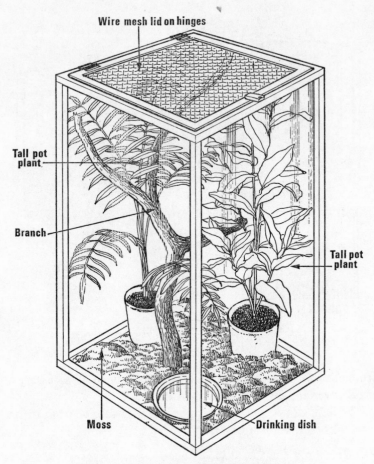

Wire mesh lid on hinges

Tall pot plant

Branch

Tall pot plant

Moss

Drinking dish

Fig 8   Tree-frog and chameleon cage

much larger following, some aquarists adopt a more ambitious way of keeping their charges, and make use of a fish-house. Similarly, a herpetologist can use his conservatory, greenhouse, garden shed, or even balcony. Provided that there are no escape holes, and there is access to water and hiding places, various species of lizards, tortoises and terrapins, frogs, toads and tree-frogs, can be kept in such ample surroundings. There must, of course, be some control over excess heat or frost. A heater may

26

become necessary during a cold spell. In very warm weather the door or window can be replaced with a frame of fine-mesh wire netting.

Detailed instructions are not necessary, as the owner will adapt whatever is available to suit his collection. The author's conservatory, where his aqua-terrarium was housed, was modified in this manner. In the freedom of the room itself, lived a tortoise or two, tree-frogs which clung to the vine, geckos and various small lizards, as well as a very friendly young crocodile and a python. Since heat was cut off during winter the tropical species were then brought indoors.

Since this room was in constant use during summer, for meals and rest periods, humans were in frequent attendance. Many an amusing incident occurred when guests were present for the first time, and viewed the scene with some trepidation. It is in this manner that a herpetologist can promote his hobby, and even encourage a more rational and healthier approach towards his pets, by relieving the uninitiated of unnecessary fears and prejudices. Neighbours' children, in particular, were in constant attendance, but were asked to contribute food as a kind of 'entrance fee' to the collection. This helped considerably towards the food bill!

OUTDOOR VIVARIA

There is little doubt that an outdoor enclosure, whether small or large, is to be preferred to one indoors. The animals will tend to live more naturally. Lack of a garden, or the tropical nature of the specimens, may prevent this, except during warm summer weather, when even a balcony can be brought into use. Fresh air and direct sunshine will benefit the reptiles. There is also more chance of picking up natural food in a garden enclosure, and breeding is more likely to occur. Indeed, it appears that the breeding cycle of temperate species may be interrupted if kept under indoor conditions, especially when proper hibernation cannot take place in warm surroundings. The author has frequently noticed that many species which are kept active

27

during winter fail to breed the following spring. On the other hand an indoor enclosure has one advantage: it gives greater opportunity for closer inspection and contact with the animals.

The Reptiliary (Fig 9)

Described simply, this is a piece of ground surrounded by a suitable barrier in which reptiles and amphibians are kept, and is a common feature of most zoos and reptile institutes. Many field centres, schools and museums with gardens now maintain a reptiliary for educational purposes.

There are a number of temperate species which can exist in such a place all the year round. Those which are diurnal can be watched from a hidden viewpoint, in order to study their habits. Various snakes, lizards, tortoises and terrapins have been confined by the author in this way, and a considerable amount of first-hand knowledge gained about their behaviour.

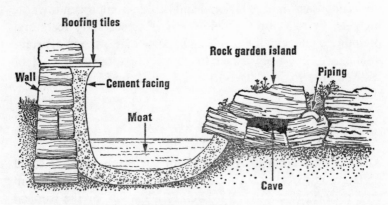

Fig 9   Reptiliary

The layout and construction will depend on cost, labour and space available. Choose a corner where the sun can reach the enclosure during part of the day, especially during the morning. The barrier should be at least 4ft high, and built of bricks, breeze blocks, or metal sheeting. An inner overhang along the top is necessary, and can be provided by using roofing slates or tiles. To complete the job, line the inner face with a layer of

28

concrete, reinforced with wire netting, as shown in the diagram. This continues inwards to form a circular moat. The earth removed from this is piled in the centre, in the form of an island. This can be built into a rock garden.

Before placing the rocks and plants in position, one or two underground caves, made out of bricks or rocks, should be excavated, using some clay piping for entrance tunnels. The whole is then covered in, leaving an opening where the pipe reaches the surface. These caves will make ideal retreats at night, and even during hibernation, well away from frost. Make sure that there is no risk of water-logging.

Such a reptiliary will enhance the garden, and provide endless interest and instruction for the owner.

The Terrapin Enclosure (Fig 10)

A number of species of terrapin can exist outdoors in our northern climate, and will benefit from sunshine in which they can bask for hours, as they usually do in the wild. The reptiliary just described would suit them, but a far better layout is a pool

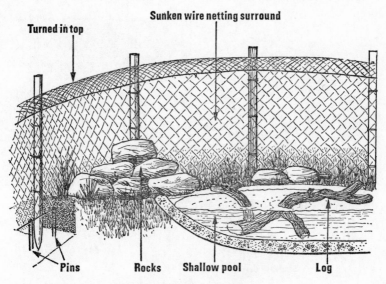

Fig 10 Terrapin enclosure

29

or small pond with an island in the centre. Terrapins usually keep out of harm's way by basking away from the bankside. Also, they usually feed in water, and retire there during dull weather and during winter. Hibernation under water is common.

A less elaborate retaining wall can be made of stout wire netting, turned inwards at the top, and supported on stakes. The bottom of the netting is firmly staked down a few inches below soil level, as described for the tortoise enclosure (Fig 11). The pond could be made out of concrete, or bought ready-made in polythene. However, the latter has a slippery surface and terrapins may have difficulty in climbing out, unless some kind of stepping stone of rock or a branch or two is included. All that is required for the island is a piece of log or a large rock to stand just above the water surface. The terrapins will crawl out and bask on this.

The Tortoise Pen (Fig 11)
Tortoises which are sold as pets are usually sufficiently hardy

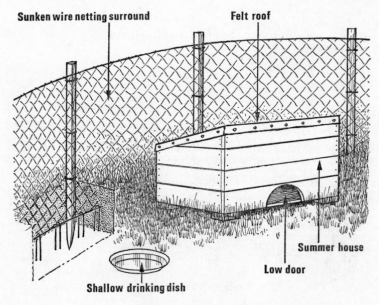

Fig 11   Tortoise pen

30

Box frame

Wire netting

Branches, sheltering places and water dish

Fig 12   Lizard cage

to live outdoors in a temperate summer climate, where the sunshine very necessary for good health can be enjoyed. A fence of stout wire netting, supported on stakes, is firmly pegged into the ground a little below the surface, with wire pins, as shown in the diagram. The height should be about 3ft. There should be no need to turn in the top edge, as may be necessary with terrapins which can climb more easily.

A summer house placed inside the enclosure will serve as a retreat during dull and rainy weather, and at night, but not for hibernation. It should be weatherproofed with a good resistant paint, and the sloping roof covered with roofing felt. The entrance must be at ground level, but the floor can be raised slightly off the ground to help keep it dry. Place the house in a sheltered corner of the pen, so as to avoid over-heating in hot weather, with the door facing south to catch the morning sun. In the author's case the summerhouse is under an over-hanging rhododendron bush.

Contrary to popular belief, most tortoises do not live in grassland and lush surroundings, but mainly in dry, almost desert, rocky areas. The soil should be loose and sandy, and contain a few flat rocks to simulate semi-desert conditions.

The Lizard Cage (Fig 12)
If kept permanently in artificial light, and away from sunshine, many lizards suffer from a vitamin deficiency. The fortunate ones benefit from the sunray treatment commonly in use in zoos and reptile houses, but direct sunlight is nature's best medicine. Even glass is a disadvantage, since it filters out the ultra-violet rays.

A reptiliary would allow lizards to bask. If this is inconvenient, a temporary home can be cheaply and easily constructed. It merely consists of a box-frame of wood covered with wire netting. This is placed, open end down, in a convenient spot such as the lawn or herbaceous border. If the wood is painted green or brown, it should not look out of place. From time to time it can be moved to a new position. A few sheltering places such as bark and rockwork, as well as branches, is all that is

Page 33   (*above*) The author's garden enclosure for tortoises, showing wire-netting surround and summerhouse; (*below*) Indian Crocodile (*Crocodylus palustris*). Young crocodilians may be kept as pets, but large specimens are best confined to zoos

required, except for a sunken water-dish. Natural food such as various insects and other garden invertebrates will no doubt enter this cage, and provide additional food for the inmates.

This enclosure is exposed to all weather conditions, and this will have to be watched. It is only a summer home, and not really suitable for winter conditions.

The Garden Pond (Fig 13)
Garden lovers who own a pond, and keep the usual goldfish swimming among the waterlilies, may view with mixed feelings the suggestion that it can also be used to encourage certain amphibians and reptiles to live and breed, and provide an excellent outdoor 'classroom' in the study of pond life generally.

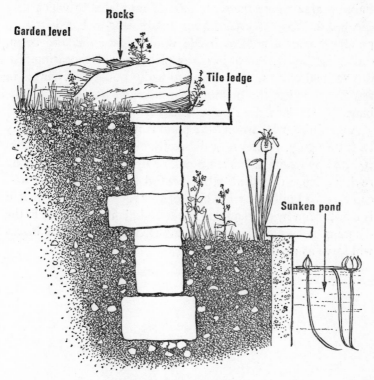

Fig 13   Garden pond

The author's pond, a modest 15ft × 6ft attracts a yearly influx of frogs, toads and newts which have freedom to come and go. The goldfish, contrary to general belief, are seldom molested, and the mixed community seems to thrive well. The odd goldfish fry may disappear, the victim of a newt, but tables are turned when a goldfish swallows a tadpole. On balance the numbers are usually maintained, as is nature's way in controlling populations. For example, it is estimated that, out of some 4,000 eggs laid in one clump of spawn by a Common Frog (*Rana temporaria*), probably no more than a half-dozen will reach maturity as frogs.

The person who owns a pond may not realise that he is helping the conservation-minded herpetologist to keep a local population of amphibians from extinction, especially in a built-up area where there are next to no places in which they can breed. Water is essential for amphibians to breed in, so a pond becomes a nucleus inside what might otherwise be an ecological desert. Ponds in many places are disappearing fast, due to neglect or filling in, or are badly polluted. Changes in farming practice, the building of roads and houses, or disturbance by children, are further hazards.

A confining wall around the pond is not necessary, and may look unsightly. However, a discreetly hidden wall can be constructed by having a sunken pond, or by building an encircling rock garden, in itself an attractive foil to the water. The wall can then be built along the base of this rock garden, so that it is half-hidden by overhanging rocks and plants, as shown in the diagram. A row of roofing tiles inserted in between the bricks will serve as an overhang.

CHAPTER 2

Food for Amphibians and Reptiles

IN deciding what to give one's pet to eat, it is a good idea to study its natural habitat, to see what food is likely to turn up there. This can then be obtained from the site—maybe from the garden—or supplied by culture or from the pet shop. For example, a slow-worm living on a rubbish dump would have a good supply of earthworms and slugs to hand. These could be found in the garden compost heap. A desert Gopher Tortoise would feed naturally on cacti and plants from dry situations. These could perhaps be found on dry wasteland locally, or on a sand dune; plants like the houseleek (*Sempervivum tectorum*) are usually tempting. A King Snake which hunts small mammals could be supplied with mice from the pet shop; in the author's case, supply is through a helpful friend who runs an animal house at a research centre.

One serious warning: never feed a reptile or amphibian just prior to hibernation. The meal may not get properly digested, but go bad in the animal's stomach, and cause death.

The following is a list of various foodstuffs, and how to obtain and culture them:

Water algae
These simplest of green plants include many one-celled and filamentous forms, and occur in most ponds and standing water, from puddles to lakes. They can be cultured in any available container, such as a bucket, bowl, water-butt or water-trough standing outside. In the spore stage they are conveyed by wind, or they can be introduced by adding pond water or water plants to which they adhere. To encourage growth, add some milk, garden fertiliser or meat extract. In

sunlight the algae will benefit from this food supply. It is the one-celled plants that cause the water to turn green. Filamentous algae, sometimes called pond-scums or blanket-weed, can be gathered from most ponds. This is food for both frog and toad tadpoles.

Infusoria

This old Victorian word refers to the aquatic life which results from an 'infusion' such as hay or lettuce leaves steeped in water. The bacteria which cause this decay supply food for many one-celled animals (Protozoa) which, in turn, can be fed to baby amphibian larvae such as newts and salamanders, also *Xenopus*, the African aquatic frogs.

One method of culture is to boil some wheat, rice or oat grains in water, strain into jars or bowls and allow to stand. Then add some pond water. Alternatives which can be added to natural water are boiled egg-yolk, meat extract, or baby food.

The already mentioned steeped hay, or horse manure, will produce good results. The idea is to get a good culture of bacteria going, on which the introduced protozoans will feed and thrive.

Earthworms

Earthworms or Oligochaeta are segmented worms which inhabit the soil, freshwater and sea. Bristle-like hairs, the *chaetae*, protrude from the skin. They are hermaphrodite and lay eggs. Earthworms come to the surface at night, or after rain, in order to mate or to drag food such as leaves into their burrows. Worm casts are a good sign of where to find them. To approach and catch one by hand is not easy—only the song-thrush seems adept at this! One method is to go out after dark with a torch; the light from this seems to arrest their movement and they can be picked up. Another way is to insert a fork into the lawn and tap the handle; the vibrations caused will bring them to the surface. Plain digging is hard work, but can produce results. Worms often turn up under stones, logs and other objects.

A compost heap is a good attraction to encourage a gathering of earthworms. Kitchen waste such as peelings, vegetable leaves, tea leaves, and so on, can be put down in a spare corner on the garden soil, and covered with some wet sacking.

The earthworm is valuable food for many amphibians and reptiles, quite apart from its use to the fisherman. One type of worm should be avoided as it seems to contain poisonous properties: the Brandling Worm (*Eisenia foetida*), which grows to about 4½in. It is banded in rings of yellow and red-brown, and usually turns up in rich manure.

Aquatic worms

There are a number of useful 'worms', to use the term loosely, found in fresh water. The Sludge Worm (*Tubifex*), is a small, segmented worm related to the earthworm, and occurs in mud along the borders of rivers, lakes and ponds, particularly in estuaries and in outflows of sewage. It constructs a tube in the mud, and dense masses may be seen, waving their bodies from their tubes, giving the mud a reddish tint. The 'Blood-worm' is the larval stage of a midge, *Chironomus*, which lays eggs in jelly-masses at the water's edge. It can be seen on the supports of piers, on boats, and along the sides of neglected swimming pools. The larvae hatch and drop to the mud. Like *Tubifex*, Blood-worms wave their bodies about, collecting food by sweeping the water with their bristle-like attachments. Many are blood-red in colour.

Both these worms may be gathered by scooping up mud and straining it under the tap in an old stocking or muslin bag. They keep for some days in clean water. Samples can sometimes be purchased at pet or bait shops. They are excellent food for newts, salamanders and their larvae.

White-worms

The white-worm (*Enchytraeus albidus*) is a small, whitish, terrestrial worm commonly found in soil and which feeds on decayed matter. It is a favourite food among aquarists for rearing fish-fry and can be easily cultured. Supplies are also available through the pet trade. To stimulate the growth of these worms, a piece of bread soaked in milk is placed in a box of loose soil and glass is laid on top. The whole should then be kept in a cool and dark place. These worms are ideal food for baby amphibians.

Water fleas and their allies
These world-wide, small crustaceans occur quite commonly in fresh water, and can be caught with a fine-meshed net. The actual water flea (family Daphnidae) gets its name from its jerky movements as it swims in the water; it is not, however, a true flea, which is an insect. Under a lens its body appears to be flattened sideways and enclosed in a transparent bivalve shell; its second pair of antennae are feathered and are used in swimming and sweeping-in food.

During the summer, only females are found. They produce in a brood-pouch nothing but daughters through a kind of virgin birth (parthenogenesis). Towards autumn, or during drought, males appear and mate with the females. Eggs are then laid in thick capsules and lie dormant until favourable weather conditions prevail. Sometimes a pond or even a puddle is swarming with *Daphnia*, turning the water a reddish brown. A relative, *Cyclops*, has a pear-shaped body and a forked and feathery tail, its long antennae are used in swimming. A pair of brood-pouches, looking like bags, are attached to the rear end of the female. Another common crustacean, *Cypris*, may appear in some ponds. Its oval, unsegmented body is laterally compressed in a bivalve shell. The eggs are laid on water plants.

These three are but a few of the many small water animals which may be collected with a pond net, or cultured at home in a water container which is well supplied with the bacteria and algae on which they feed. Prepare a ferment as described for the algae and infusoria cultures above, then add the crustaceans. This is a staple food, sometimes available in pet and aquarium shops, which can be fed to newts and salamanders in their water stage.

Water shrimp and water louse
These two larger freshwater crustaceans, readily identifiable by

40

eye, make useful food for water salamanders, terrapins, small crocodilians and some aquatic frogs.

The Water Shrimp (*Gammarus*), which is related to sand-hoppers found on the beach, is a freshwater occupant of well-oxygenated streams, and is usually hidden among water plants. It can be gathered by driving a fine net upstream through the plants. It has an arched body, flattened sideways. The Freshwater Louse (*Asellus*), is more a scavenger on the bottom of ditches and ponds, and feeds on debris and rotten leaves. Its body is flattened.

Mosquitoes, their larvae and pupae
Mosquitoes and gnats are synonymous terms for a group of insects which suck up liquid food, in some cases blood, and may transmit diseases such as malaria. Mostly they lay eggs on water; these then hatch into larvae which hang from the surface so that they can breathe air. The comma-shaped pupae, called 'tumblers' in America, are just as active. From these, usually on the water surface, emerge the adults. During summer months it is an easy matter to collect these larvae and pupae with a fine-meshed net, from almost any stagnant water.

Mosquitoes can be encouraged to breed in a water-butt or trough (provided that the neighbours do not object!) and make fine food for aquatic newts and salamanders. Frogs and toads will also benefit by catching the adults which visit a garden pond, and will help to discourage this nuisance. Obviously, mosquito encouragement should not be attempted in malaria-ridden areas.

Flies and maggots
This vast group of two-winged insects includes the familiar House-fly and the Bluebottle, both of which are a common nuisance in houses during summer. On the other hand they make excellent food for frogs and toads, also chameleons and lizards, either as larvae (maggots) or as adults.

The adults can be caught by using a fly-trap—a wire-mesh contraption, with a conical aperture beneath, which is placed over a piece of raw meat or fish. Flies which are attracted tend to leave by crawling through the conical entrance, and so get

41

trapped. They can then be released into the vivarium or cage. In the interests of health, this trap should be placed well away from the house.

Pieces of raw meat left in the open soon become fly-blown, and the maggots which hatch will provide a further food supply.

The fruit-fly (Drosophila)

This small insect is attracted to fruit, and often hangs around dustbins. Because of its size it is ideal food for baby frogs and toads.

It can be bred in the following manner. Prepare a thickening medium, such as agar or gelatine mixed with water, heat it to dissolve, and add some treacle or fruit juice. Pour this into a glass container with a narrow neck, such as a bottle, and insert a roll of blotting paper. This will soak up the mixture and attract these small flies. A few should be put in before covering the bottle-opening with muslin, they should then breed on this mixture.

Much genetical research has been carried out on this fly, and a supply may be available from a laboratory.

CHAPTER 3

The Care of Amphibians and Reptiles

As well as providing suitable living conditions for animals kept in confinement, it is necessary to know something about their general habits and needs, their correct feeding, and the pitfalls to avoid if they are to live in a healthy and breeding condition whilst in captivity. An experienced zoo keeper once told the author that success in keeping a captive animal depends on whether it feeds regularly, and also breeds—two of the essential needs of living. Some of the points to bear in mind if this is to become possible are given in this chapter; further, more specific advice is given in Chapters 5-9 after each species description.

FROGS AND TOADS

Temperature Temperate species can be kept at normal temperature and allowed to hibernate. Some frogs will do so under water. Others, and most toads, usually hibernate on land, in some hidden spot away from frost. Tropical species require permanent heating at 70–80° F.

Sunlight Direct sunlight and dry surroundings should be avoided for most species, which keep to moist and shady habitats. Some may be permanently aquatic, and require an aquarium or pond.

Feeding Frog and toad tadpoles grow up on a plant diet, whereas most adults are carnivorous, catching a variety of small animals with their tongues. A monotonous diet should be avoided. Live foods, such as meal-worms and fly maggots, can be obtained from dealers, but this should be supplemented with the many invertebrates which exist in the garden or countryside, eg earthworms, molluscs, crustaceans and spiders. Tame specimens may take pieces of raw meat held in forceps and waved about slowly in front of them.

Drinking As such this does not apply, since amphibians do not drink in the accepted sense; moisture is taken in through the skin. A dish of water must always be available, or the vivarium sprayed from time to time.

Sloughing This takes place at regular intervals, usually without any trouble. Assistance may be required in the form of moistening the skin and gently removing the outer layer, where it is stuck, with blunt forceps.

Ailments Apart from physical injury such as sores and abrasions, especially on the nose, caused by friction against a rough surface, there are more serious complaints due to bacterial or fungal attacks. These can result from poor health or polluted surroundings. The infected part should be treated with merchurochrome or an aniline dye. In the aquatic stage some specimens may suffer from a type of oedema, in which the limbs or body swell up. A salt bath, the cure recommended for fish with swim-bladder trouble, may help.

Handling This should be done as little as possible, and then only with wetted fingers. The skin is sensitive to the touch. It is better to use a net.

NEWTS AND SALAMANDERS

The general care of these amphibians is broadly similar to that for frogs and toads.

Temperature Since most species belong to temperate latitudes they can be kept at normal temperatures, and allowed to hibernate. Avoid bright light and direct sunshine.

Feeding Newts and salamanders are carnivorous, and will take various invertebrates such as earthworms, molluscs, insects and, in the aquatic stage, tadpoles, water fleas (*Daphnia*), and small pieces of raw meat. If the latter food is given, be careful not to cause pollution. The larvae also feed on animal life (see page 56).

44

Drinking See frogs and toads.

Sloughing See frogs and toads.

Ailments Loss of fingers and toes and similar injuries may occur when hungry specimens snap at each other during feeding. Such injuries usually heal and the member may even regrow. Fungal infections due to lowered resistance or polluted surroundings can rapidly spread, and should be treated as for frogs and toads.

Handling See frogs and toads.

SNAKES

Temperature Temperate species may be kept at normal temperatures. An average summer temperature of 75° F is suitable, and can be maintained during winter, provided that the specimen is fed throughout. Alternatively, remove it to a cool spot away from frost, eg in an unheated shed, garage or cellar. Tins or boxes with perforated lids, firmly secured, can be used, if they contain some dry leaves or moss. Tropical species will require constant warmth at 75–80° F.

Sunlight Sunlight is beneficial to those snakes which bask, but they should never be exposed for too long. Even a snake or lizard can die from sunstroke. The ultra-violet lamp is beneficial. Snakes, such as the large constrictors, which normally live in shady forest surroundings, appear to be less in need of direct sunlight.

Feeding Snakes can be fed about once a week—the practice normally carried out in reptile houses. At first it may be necessary to offer living prey, but most specimens soon settle down to confinement and will readily accept freshly killed food. Temperamental specimens may be encouraged by first giving them a warm bath, or by raising the cage temperature. Others can be duped by twitching a dead mouse with a thin stick, to simulate live movement, arousing the snake's interest.

Most of the water snakes feed on cold-blooded prey (frogs, toads, newts, fish). Garter Snakes will also take earthworms.

Small mammals and birds are accepted by most of the Colubrids. Domestic mice can be provided, and rats or rabbits for larger specimens such as the constrictors. A supply of dead mice and rats can be kept in cold storage and thawed out when required; or a collection can be kept and bred by the owner. Sometimes a leg or part of the body of a mouse or rat will be taken.

When food is short, various techniques can be tried to induce feeding. The author managed by rubbing a live frog on some raw meat. This was accepted by a Grass-snake (*Natrix*). With a reluctant King Snake (*Lampropeltis*), scent of a dead mouse was rubbed in a similar manner, and the piece of meat immediately taken and swallowed. Another method is to skin a frog or mouse and fill it with minced meat. To this can be added a useful tablet of cod-liver oil as a tonic. Snakes rely much on scent and recognise their prey through this sense. As proof the author once tried an experiment, by transferring the scent of a rat to a small rubber toy. A python then tried to swallow it!

Forced feeding should only be attempted as a last resort. It is easy to damage a snake's delicate jaw mechanism. Raw egg mixed with milk or cod-liver oil is better than a solid meal. It can be administered with a syringe of the kind used for filling car batteries. Hold the snake firmly behind the neck, and gently rub the side of its mouth with the nozzle. As the mouth opens, insert the nozzle down its throat and slowly pump the syringe contents into its stomach.

Drinking Snakes drink frequently, but do not seem to like milk. When freshly caught or acquired, they will drink more readily than they will feed. The mouth is inserted into the water in the way a horse drinks. A small pan of water, always fresh and clean, should be available at all times, especially during periods of absence. A snake can go without food for many weeks, but must have drinking water available.

Sloughing A clean and entire slough means a healthy snake. When the skin comes away in shreds, and pieces stick to the body, wrap the snake in a damp cloth for a few hours—tying

46

up in a linen bag would do. The softened skin can then be peeled away gently with blunt tweezers.

Note: a good time to feed a snake is immediately after it has sloughed.

Ailments If properly cared for, snakes are usually free from ailments. However, these do occur, usually due to wrong management or neglect. One of the commonest complaints is bacterial or fungal infection: one type, called mouth canker, attacks the gums and tissue of the mouth, even the bones, and appears as a cheesy substance which may lead to death. The cause is not known, but could be starvation and lowered resistance, or injury of the mouth or teeth, perhaps from abrasions where the nose has been rubbed raw in attempts to escape. Also, too large a meal can upset digestion and cause a blockage. In attempts to disgorge, damage can result. Patience and daily treatment is necessary. Remove all dead tissue, broken teeth and yellow matter. Give the mouth a daily spray with a mild antiseptic or antibiotic diluted in water. Treatment may have to continue for a month or more. Little is known about the value of antibiotics or sulpha drugs on cold-blooded animals, but their use seems justified in attempting to save the life of a valued snake.

Various mites will occasionally attack captive snakes, but seem rare in wild specimens. When they bite, a blood disease is sometimes transmitted, and usually proves fatal. This has happened even in well-kept reptile houses, and the disease has spread from cage to cage. It is always wise to carefully inspect any new arrival, and to keep it in quarantine for a while. The author once lost his entire collection by carelessly introducing an infected snake purchased from a pet shop. A sign of this blood disease is the manner in which a snake gapes with its mouth and rubs its body against the cage. Treatment is to remove any visible mites with tweezers, better still to immerse the snake in soapy water for a while. The body can also be wiped with a soapy cloth. The cage may have to be cleared and thoroughly washed with a detergent containing a disinfectant. Allow it to dry before returning the occupants.

Ticks, if they occur, can be removed with tweezers, afterwards treating the spot with an antiseptic ointment to clean and sterilise the wound.

Handling Unless it is already tame, or has been given time to settle into its new home, a snake should not be handled. There is a certain art in doing so. Snakes do not have to be gripped or held as one might hold a kitten, but should be allowed to rest on the hand or along the arm. One hand can hold the body loosely, but allow the coils free movement. The snake should soon settle down and appear to enjoy the warmth of human contact. Some, like constrictors and climbing snakes, will grip the hand or arm, using it as a support as if it were a tree with branches.

A note of warning: never take liberties with venomous snakes. They may appear to be tame, but one can never be sure. Sooner or later most herpetologists get bitten, due to carelessness or over-confidence. Always wear stout leather gloves, or use a hooked stick.

LIZARDS

Temperature As with snakes, temperature extremes should be avoided. Temperate species can be hibernated as for snakes (page 45), but tropical specimens will need constant warmth. The general treatment is the same for both reptiles.

Sunlight This is important, even more so for lizards than for snakes. The reason has to do with the supply of vitamins. It has been suggested that snakes derive them from their food, from such prey as mammals and birds. With most lizards this source is lacking, since they feed largely on invertebrates such as insects. In their case the 'sun' vitamin, D, is derived from the sun's ultra-violet rays. Since most glass filters out these rays, direct contact is necessary. The UV lamp is a valuable asset; alternatively the specimens can be placed outdoors in an open lizard cage during warm and sunny spells (see page 31).

Feeding This varies with the species, but usually consists of various insects, crustaceans, earthworms, spiders in particular, and grasshoppers. Large specimens will take small mammals. Some are vegetarian. Raw meat can also be tried.

Drinking Always have a supply of fresh drinking water available. Lizards lap up water in the way a cat does. Tree climbers such as anoles and chameleons lap up drops of water from leaves covered with rain-water or dew. This can be supplied by an occasional spray.

Sloughing See snakes. Lizards usually lose their outer skin in pieces.

Ailments All fresh specimens, especially those purchased from dealers, should be examined for external parasites such as mites or ticks. Mouth canker may also develop: treat as for snakes. Swellings on the body may also develop as growths, usually due to malnutrition and lack of vitamins. Some growths can be removed with a sharp knife and the wound treated with an antiseptic. Sunlight and a varied diet are the best preventives. Bone softening causes a condition resembling rickets and again is caused by a monotonous diet and calcium deficiency. Add grated cuttlefish bone or bone-meal to the diet, and an occasional dose of cod-liver oil.

Handling Take great care not to hold a lizard by its tail; in many species this easily fractures. Hold loosely in the hand— most species will hang on to the hand or clothing anyway. Gloves may be required in handling large specimens, or freshly caught lizards. A bite, although painful, is not usually serious.

Note: only the two American lizards, the Gila Monster and the Mexican Beaded Lizard, are venomous.

ALLIGATORS AND CROCODILES

Temperature A water temperature of 75–80° F is recommended, but can be lowered during the winter for northerly species, such as the Mississippi Alligator, which hibernates in its native home. Caimans and crocodiles from the more tropical regions are best kept warm all year round.

Sunlight This is very beneficial, as these reptiles bask a lot.

They can all be kept outdoors during warm and sunny weather.

Feeding To some degree crocodilians are scavengers, and will eat almost anything of animal origin, provided that it is not too bad. Raw meat, fish, frogs, crayfish, dead rats and birds, should all be given to make a varied diet. Do not give salty or cured food. Grated cuttle-bone or bone-meal can be added. If forced feeding is necessary, use a blunt wooden rod to push the food gently down the throat. To avoid pollution, food should not be left lying about. These animals are creatures of habit: some will eat on land, others in water, so place the food in the same spot each time. Since they will snap at food, it is wise not to feed by hand.

Drinking This happens automatically when the animals enter or feed in water.

Sloughing This is not very noticeable. From time to time the odd outer scale will come off.

Ailments Some specimens may develop sores on the snout due to rubbing against their enclosure. Sharp stones and similar hazards should be avoided. Treat sores and cuts with a mild antiseptic and keep clean. Beware of polluted water. Cuttle-bone added to food will help to avoid calcium deficiency which may lead to bone softening.

Handling Young specimens, which are the ones usually kept as pets, seem to tame readily, but gloves may be necessary. In handling a specimen, grasp it around the body just behind the forelegs with one hand and grip the tail firmly with the other. Most of the strength lies in the tail.

TERRAPINS

Temperature Temperate specimens can be kept at normal temperatures, and even allowed to hibernate. Water species will hibernate under water; some, like the mud turtles, buried in mud. Avoid any risk from frost. Tropical species require a constant warm temperature.

Sunlight This is very beneficial, almost essential, in maintaining

Page 51　Edible Frog (*Rana esculenta*). A pair of a species widely known throughout Europe. The smaller male (left) is highly vocal

Page 52 (*above*) Mexican Axolotl (*Siredon mexicanum*). A survivor of two winters in a garden pond, this aquarium specimen has bred successfully three times; (*below*) Clawed Toad (*Xenopus laevis*). This primitive, aquatic amphibian is so named because of the claws on its hind feet

good health, especially in baby specimens. Keep outside in warm and sunny weather if at all possible.

Feeding This varies with the species, but is mainly small animals caught in water such as aquatic insects, snails, tadpoles and small fish, and occasional plants. To these can be added pieces of raw fish and meat. Box turtles will eat both plant and animal food.

Drinking Does not apply, since it occurs when the terrapin is in water.

Sloughing Parts of the outer shell flake off from time to time, and usually give little trouble.

Ailments Occasional external parasites such as ticks and leeches may be removed with blunt tweezers, and the spot treated with a mild antiseptic. Fungus sores can be cured with a salt wash. Lack of sunlight, especially in babies, may lead to serious trouble such as blindness and ultimate death. Shell softening is probably a sign of calcium deficiency. Add grated cuttle-bone to the food, also cod-liver oil. Never paint the shell, especially in youngsters, as this hinders growth. It is a stupid habit and to be discouraged.

Handling Hold by the shell. Gloves may be necessary if the specimen is likely to bite, but this is unusual once the animal is used to handling.

TORTOISES

Temperature Normal temperature can be maintained for temperate species, which can be allowed to hibernate. This includes the Mediterranean species and the American box turtles and gophers. Place in a box filled with dry leaves or hay and cover the open top with wire netting or sacking, firmly secured to prevent escapes. Place in a cold but frost-free position (see Snakes, page 45). Tropical species require constantly warm surroundings.

Sunlight As much as possible but, if the specimen is kept outdoors, provide a shelter to retire into at night, during rain or excessive sunshine.

D   53

Feeding Land tortoises are mainly vegetarian. A variety of greenstuff and fruit can be given, and occasional animal food may be tried. Box turtles will eat both.

Drinking Much of a tortoise's moisture requirement comes from the plant food. A shallow dish of fresh water should always be available. An occasional warm bath of shallow water is beneficial, and may induce a reluctant tortoise to feed. Food can be dipped in water before it is offered.

Sloughing From time to time an outer scale will flake off. The shell can be kept in good condition by an occasional wash in soapy water, and rubbing with olive oil.

Ailments If present, ticks can be removed with blunt tweezers. First soften the area with a drop of spirits so that the tick loosens its hold, and treat the spot afterwards with a mild disinfectant. Cracked shell or other injuries, such as cuts and sores, should be treated and kept clean.

CHAPTER 4

Rearing Young

ONE satisfactory achievement in any pet hobby is the successful breeding of young, and the pleasure of helping to raise a family. Breeding has been commonplace for many years as part of the fish-aquarium hobby, so much so that a number of fish have, over the centuries, become domesticated by selective breeding. The goldfish is an example. With the vivarium hobby, breeding is still in its infancy, and no amphibian or reptile can be called truly domestic; although tame as pets they are still wild animals —a point sometimes overlooked. This applies even to the placid tortoise. Breeding can prove a challenge to the owner, but with proper care and surroundings there can be success in this interesting pastime.

AMPHIBIANS

In most cases some sort of water container is required as a breeding site. A pond would be ideal, and most temperate species will breed in this. Tropical amphibians require warm, indoor conditions. With newts and the smaller salamanders which enter water to breed, the aquarium is quite suitable, and the author has had a number of successes. Larger individuals, as well as most frogs and toads, require more space, ie the outdoor pond or some large indoor water container. The author made use of a spare bath in his study (to the consternation of the family!), and managed to breed from a pair of Bullfrogs (*Rana catesbiana*), sent from America by a friend.

Once the eggs have been laid, or young produced as the case may be, they should at once be removed to a separate 'nursery'

—a tank of shallow water in which to metamorphose. In confined space there is apt to be some cannibalism by the adults, particularly with newts.

Tadpoles of frogs and toads are equipped with larval teeth and will browse on water plants, in particular the algae which grow on underwater sticks and stones, other plants, and even on the aquarium glass. To these can be added the leaves of lettuce, nettle and spinach. Dip these in boiling water to soften first. As legs appear, many tadpoles tend to become scavengers, eating at almost any sick or dead water animal. The author has known them to attack sickly goldfish in his pond. Pieces of raw meat attached to a cotton thread can be lowered into the tank and, when finished with, pulled out so as to avoid pollution. The *Xenopus* tadpoles, however, are filter-feeders and will require supplies of infusoria and water algae to feed on.

At the time of emergence a floating piece of wood will suffice as a temporary raft on which to climb. The youngsters can then be transferred to a land vivarium as is shown in Figs 1A, 2 or 6. Under pond conditions outdoors they will emerge normally, and wander off to take their chance in the garden.

Newt and salamander tadpoles start life as animal feeders, and as they grow should be given a graduated diet, starting with infusoria, then changing to small animal life such as water fleas, blood-worms, *Tubifex* and mosquito larvae. In an outdoor pond these should occur naturally. At metamorphosis they can be treated as for baby frogs and toads, and placed in the vivarium.

Once transformed, none of these youngsters are too easy to rear. Patience and time is required to find and supply a regular diet of small invertebrates. Greenfly, *Drosophila*, *Enchytraeus*, tiny earthworms, small insects and their larvae, are suggested. Rearing a frog, toad or salamander from babyhood can become a labour of love, but can also give much satisfaction.

Eggs laid by reptiles can be left where they are, provided that the heat source is maintained. In temperate lands the eggs are deposited in some spot which receives constant warmth from the sun, or from fermenting vegetation. In most cases a constant temperature of about 70° F, over a period of ten to twelve weeks, is necessary for the eggs to incubate and hatch. If there is any doubt about this they should be removed and placed on dampened moss or cotton wool, in a container with a perforated lid. This arrangement will provide moisture and darkness.

There are two important points to remember. Firstly, the eggs must be removed and put in the container in exactly the same position, ie without twisting. Only birds turn their eggs during incubation. If this happens with a reptile's eggs the embryos are liable to suffer and may die. Secondly, too dry a container may cause the eggs to become addled and cease development, although too much moisture may cause fungal attacks.

A suitable position for the container will suggest itself to the owner—for example a warm airing cupboard, over a radiator or, as one friend used to do, floated in a tropical aquarium. In this manner he managed to hatch out lizards, snakes and tortoises.

Once hatched the babies will require especial care and feeding. Most lizards will take small insects and molluscs, especially ants and spiders, and the litter fauna generally, also maybe small bits of raw meat. Baby terrapins can be fed on raw meat and water life (water fleas, mosquito larvae, *Tubifex*), and some species may take algae. Baby tortoises are reared on soft fruit, and plants such as lettuce, nettle, dandelion and rose leaves. Earthworms, insect larvae and raw meat can be added for box turtles. Baby snakes present a problem. Little is known about their diet in the wild, but presumably they feed on small animal prey. It is a matter of experimenting with a variety of insects, molluscs, etc. Young crocodilians are usually an easy matter, and will take small water animals such as insects or tadpoles, pieces of raw meat, in fact almost anything to hand.

57

Hibernation is a matter of choice. Personally, the author always overwinters any of these youngsters indoors for the first winter, and continues to feed them, so as to give a good start in life. But, as already mentioned, all this becomes a labour of love.

CHAPTER 5

Frogs and Toads

Family Ranidae

This is the typical and best-known family of frogs, with world-wide distribution. It includes the British Common Frog (*Rana temporaria*), as well as the world's largest, the African Goliath Frog (*Gigantorana goliath*) and America's largest, the Bullfrog (*R. catesbiana*). Many species in temperate lands tend to gather together in breeding colonies during the spring, and spawn at the same time. This is known as 'explosive' breeding. Eggs are laid by each female in clumps, called frog spawn.

Common Frog (*Rana temporaria*)

This well-known species extends from Britain right across Europe as far as Japan, and from latitude 70° N to the southern mountain ranges of Eurasia. The colour varies considerably between individuals, and changes with the surroundings, but the markings remain constant. There is a temporal patch across ear, eye and eardrum (tympanum). The male has internal vocal sacs and gives a dull croak.

This frog lives in shady and damp places in a wide range of habitats such as waste undergrowth, long grass, ditches, edges of ponds and streams, and in gardens where there are ponds. Breeding is explosive; in early March in the south but possibly as late as June in the north and in mountains. Spawn may contain up to 4,000 eggs. Tadpoles metamorphose and emerge in about June, and mature in the fourth year. Food consists of various invertebrates such as earthworms, molluscs, crustaceans, various insects and their grubs, all caught on the tongue.

Vivarium: 1A, 2, 3, 6, 9, 13. Does well in captivity. Has been kept for twelve years.

Edible Frog (Rana esculenta)
This more aquatic frog is lively in movement, and occurs in west and central Europe, from southern Sweden to France and Italy. It was introduced into Britain in the early nineteenth century, into the fens and meres of East Anglia. It is now almost extinct there. Colour is variable, but is mostly a rich brown or bright emerald, with darker markings and a pale stripe down the back. It lives in colonies in ponds, canals and along lake borders, basking at the water's edge but quickly diving in if disturbed. Breeding is more protracted than in the Common Frog, and commences late, in about May. Some 6,000 eggs are laid in scattered clumps. The male gives a loud and penetrating song by inflating the external vocal sacs at the angles of the jaw; a colony in full song is a familiar sound after rain and on warm nights over most of Europe. Food consists of most small land invertebrates, also aquatic life which can be caught under water.

Vivarium: 5, 6, 13. A pond is probably the best place, although neighbours may object to the croaking. Has been kept for six years.

Marsh or Laughing Frog (Rana ridibunda)
Some authorities consider this frog to be a separate species, others believe it is a sub-species of the Edible Frog, and call it *Rana esculenta ridibunda*. Its range is more easterly, from Germany to the Soviet Union, the Urals and parts of western Asia and north Africa. It is the largest European frog, measuring up to about 4½in. In many ways it resembles the Edible Frog on a bigger scale. It has been established in the dykes of Romney Marsh and neighbouring marshes of Kent, England, since 1935. The chorus is very loud, hence the name, *ridibunda*, which means laughing.

Vivarium: 5, 6, 13. In the author's experience these frogs, unless young, tend to wander away from a pond, preferring larger, more open water. Has been kept for six years.

American Bullfrog (Rana catesbiana)
This largest frog of America can measure up to nearly 8in, even more in the female. It extends throughout much of the United

States, east of the Rockies. Colour varies from green to greenish-brown, marked with darker spots. Highly aquatic, the Bullfrog inhabits the larger lakes and marshes, living among the water plants or basking at the water's edge. Rather solitary, it assembles in colonies for breeding during June and July. Fighting occurs among the males, whose booming cry can be heard for a long distance. It is likened to a bull's roar, and called the 'jug-o-rum' call. Its diet includes fish, crayfish, small mammals and nestlings, even snakes. Tadpoles may take up to two or three years to metamorphose.

Vivarium: 1A, 2, 3, 6, 13. Allowance must be made for its size, although a tame specimen will live quite well in a small vivarium, kept by itself. Has been kept for sixteen years.

Agile Frog (*Rana dalmatina*)

This lively species resembles *Rana temporaria,* but is more slimly built and has a more pointed snout and much longer hind-legs in proportion to its size. The toes are long and shiny. Colour is generally a light brown, with few markings. There is a large temporal patch. It ranges from southern Sweden, across France and Germany as far as the Balkans and parts of south-west Asia. The habitat is similar to that of *temporaria,* and usually lowland woods, sometimes far from water. Breeding is explosive, and during it the males croak loudly—a kind of 'ko-ko-ko' in rapid succession. Food is similar to *temporaria.*

Vivarium: 1A, 2, 3, 6, 9, 13. Has been kept for five years.

Leopard Frog (*Rana pipiens*)

This North American species, and typical representative there of the genus *Rana,* is found in the western United States, between the Sierra Nevada range and the eastern Great Plains. It is somewhat similar in shape to *R. esculenta.* Colour varies from a bright green-grey to brown, marked with irregular rows of dark spots along the back and limbs. It inhabits meadows, ditches and open woodland glades. The male gives a soft, gutteral croak. Habits are similar to those of *R. temporaria.*

Vivarium: 1A, 2, 3, 6, 9, 13. Has been kept for six years.

Family Discoglossidae
This small family is more closely related to toads (Arcifera). Its name means 'rounded tongue'. Food is caught with the mouth. There are no vocal sacs. During mating the male grips the female in amplexus around the groins. In the tadpole the gill opening (spiracle) is median.

Painted Frog (Discoglossus pictus)
This strongly built toad is usually called a frog because of its smooth skin and frog-like appearance. It can be distinguished by the small and almost invisible tympanum, sturdy fore-limbs and poorly webbed hind-feet. Colour varies, from dark-brown to grey, sometimes reddish, marked with dark-brown patches with white borders. There may be a pale dorsal stripe. This rather aquatic frog is found in marshes and pools, even in cold mountain streams, in the Iberian peninsula, southern France, Sicily, Malta and north-west Africa, spending much of the time in water with just the head showing. Spawning is intermittent. The male gives a soft 'ra-ra'.

Vivarium: 1, 5, 6, 9, 13. In shallow water.

Yellow-bellied and Fire-bellied Toads (Bombina)
The Yellow-bellied Toad (*Bombina variegata*), is a small toad, about 2in long, readily recognised by its earthy-brown to greyish body-colour. The belly and underside of the limbs are marked with yellow or orange patches, and it is blue-black in between. It ranges throughout western Europe as far east as west Germany, and southwards to the Alps, north Italy and Albania. It may occur in lowland areas but is more common in hilly country.

The Fire-bellied Toad (*B. bombina*), its close relative, is readily distinguished by its more reddish, speckled underparts. It is similar in size and build, but occurs more to the east and north, from southern Sweden and Denmark through parts of Germany to Rumania, Bulgaria, Yugoslavia and the northern parts of Asia Minor. It keeps more to the lowlands.

Both Yellow- and Fire-bellied Toads spend much of their lives in the shallow water of pools and marshes. During drought they dig into the mud or retire into holes. Mating is protracted, from April onwards, and a female may spawn several times. Males utter soft cries of 'oonk-oonk'. The bright underparts of both species serve as a 'flash mechanism' to deter an enemy. A disturbed toad will flatten its body, turn and reverse the limbs upwards to expose the colours. Testing this, the author has found that both his cat and dog have hesitated to touch the toad.

Vivarium: 5, 6 in shallow water. Both species will breed readily. Specimens have been kept for seven years.

Midwife Toad (Alytes obstetricans)
This small and interesting little toad, about 2in long, is named after its unusual habits. In build it resembles a miniature Common Toad (*Bufo bufo*). Colour is a dull shade of grey or brown, with the glands marked in black. The range is western Europe from Spain and Portugal up to Holland, and across France and Belgium to Germany and Switzerland.

This very terrestrial toad inhabits wooded country, hiding among rocks, under logs etc, concealed by day. At night the attractive call of the male can be heard—a single, repeated bell-like note, hence its other name of Bell Toad. A male may mate several times. With each female he gathers her strings of spawn and winds them around his thighs. They are carried around, moistened occasionally, until ready to hatch. The male then enters some shallow water, and the tadpoles are released. They grow to a large size, up to 1½in.

Vivarium: 1A, 2, 3, 6, 9. Has been kept for twenty years. This toad was used in the famous (or infamous) experiment to prove the Lamarkian theory of acquired characteristics, in which males kept in water were supposed to develop nuptial pads, which they never do in nature.

Family Bufonidae
As the Ranidae is for frogs, this is the typical family of toads. It includes the two British species, the Common Toad (*Bufo bufo*) and the Natterjack (*Bufo calamita*), as well as the world's largest, the American Marine Toad (*Bufo marinus*). The range

63

is world-wide. The skin is dry and warty and the parotid glands are prominent. There are no teeth.

Common Toad (Bufo bufo)
This well-known species of bufonid has a wide distribution through the whole of Europe north of the Alps, and across temporate Asia as far as Japan. An average male measures 2¾in, but some females show gigantism and can reach 8in. The fat and thickset body is covered in warts, with prominent parotids. Colour varies from grey to brown, sometimes reddish. It frequents many habitats, often far from water, in woodland, gardens, caves, and in underground places such as cellars, drains and between rocks. Breeding is explosive. Colonies gather in spring, the males usually preceding the females, and amplexus may take place before entering the water. Males produce a repeated, high-pitched croak, not unlike a puppy yapping. Since they outnumber the females there is sometimes a scramble for a mate, resulting in a 'knot of toads' with a number of males hanging on to one female. She can lay up to 7,000 eggs in long strings.

The Common Toad is passive and docile, spending long periods in one spot, to which it returns every morning after a nocturnal search for food. It has a strong homing instinct, and is known to migrate up to a mile in order to reach a certain pond, probably where it was born. Where a migration route crosses a highway many get run over. Large numbers of nocturnal insects are caught, especially ants and beetles.

Vivarium: 1A, 2, 3, 9 in fairly dry surroundings. This toad makes a delightful family pet, and tames and feeds readily. The author kept one for twelve years, and it became a television personality. Has also been kept as a gardener's ally for thirty-six years.

Natterjack (Bufo calamita)
This smaller cousin of the Common Toad occurs in west and central Europe from southern Sweden south to Spain, and from the Atlantic seaboard to Poland. In Britain it has become rare, and only occurs in a few places. It prefers habitats with loose

soil, in sand-dunes and on heathland. Size in both sexes is about 3in. Colour is olive-brown or olive-green, marbled with irregular brown spots. The warts are tipped in red. There is a sulphur-yellow stripe along the back. Hind legs are short and it tends to run along instead of hop; the old name for it was Running Toad. It is diurnal, and can be seen in loose colonies running through the sand-dunes, especially along the Atlantic coast. It burrows a lot during drought and when hibernating.

Breeding is protracted, sometimes well into summer. The male swells up its large vocal sac and produces an attractive trilling note among the reeds, hence its name (Latin, *calamus* = reed). These toads will tolerate, and spawn in, brackish water.

Vivarium: 1A, 2, 3, 9 with plenty of loose soil. Has lived for sixteen years. Since British specimens are rare, please do not collect. There are plenty on the continent.

Green Toad (*Bufo viridis*)

This toad resembles *Bufo bufo* in general build, and grows to about 3½in; the female is a little smaller. The colours are a very attractive olive-green marked with darker greenish patches. The warts are reddish. The distribution is western, central and southern Europe, also northern Africa and western Asia as far as Tibet. It takes over where *B. bufo* leaves off and is more an inhabitant of open country, such as the Asian steppes, and avoids wooded areas. It can tolerate dry conditions and frequently burrows. Breeding is protracted, and the male's croak is a melodious trill.

Vivarium: 1A, 2, 3, 9 as for *B. bufo*. Has lived for nine years.

The North American Toad (*B. terrestris*), and the north African species (*B. regularis*), have rather similar habits, and can be treated like the Common Toad (*B. bufo*). The African species, however, will require some heating during winter.

Marine Toad (*Bufo marinus*)

This, the world's largest toad, can reach a length of 9½in, and its plump and rounded body covers a saucer. It lives in northern South America, but has been introduced elsewhere, notably into Florida as well as Hawaii and Australia, as a useful ally in

65

plantations against insects. It can even catch and swallow mice. The colour is brownish to reddish-brown, and the parotids are very large. The poison emitted has been known to kill unwary dogs. Wearing gloves is perhaps advisable, although it readily becomes tame.

Vivarium: 1A, 2, 3, 9. Some warmth is advised. Has lived well in captivity for twenty years or more.

Family Pelobatidae—Spade-foot Toads
This is a family of burrowing toads, found mainly in the northern hemisphere, in America, Europe and Asia. Those more frequently seen in the vivarium are the European genus *Pelobates* and the American *Scaphiopus*. There is a broad tubercle on the inner side of each hind-foot, containing a bony core, used in digging into the soil. They may stay below ground for long periods.

Spade-foot or Garlic Toad (Pelobates fuscus)
This European species extends throughout much of Europe from France eastwards to the Urals, and south to the Alps, Balkans and Caucasus. A slightly larger species, *P. cultripes*, lives in the Iberian peninsula, southern France and Morocco. The size of *fuscus* is about 2½in. It has a thickset body, rather hump-shaped, and a smooth skin. The male has large glands on each upper arm, and these can emit a garlic odour, but has no vocal sacs or thumb pads. Colour is some shade of grey, yellow or brown, marbled with olive-brown or brick-red. The eye-pupil is vertical. Breeding is protracted and the female deposits short, thick strings of spawn at intervals. Tadpoles develop slowly and can grow to more than 6½in, the largest in Europe. They may take up to two years to develop.

Vivarium: 1A, 2, 3, 9. Requires plenty of loose, preferably damp, soil in which to burrow. It does not often come into view. *P. fuscus* has been kept for nine years.

The American Spade-foot Toad (*Scaphiopus holbrookii*), from the eastern United States is much the same as its European cousin, spending a good deal of time burrowed below ground.

Family Hylidae—Tree-toads

Although usually referred to as tree-frogs, these amphibians are more closely related to toads (Arcifera). All are confined to the New World, except for the typical genus *Hyla* which ranges world-wide, and is mostly kept in vivaria. The true tree-frogs (family Polypedatidae), are tropical and belong to the Old World. Most live above ground, in bushes and trees, and some lay their eggs on leaves suspended over water. Others beat the water into a froth which forms a hard shell inside which the eggs can develop. Outside their native range, they do not normally breed, and, in the author's opinion, are not very successful in a vivarium.

A note of caution here: some of these hylids can be very noisy, especially at night and during wet weather. If kept indoors, they can be quite disturbing to the human occupants, as the author has found to his cost.

European tree-frog (*Hyla arborea*)

This is a small species, about 2in long in both sexes, with a somewhat frog-like appearance. The smooth shiny skin varies much in colour according to surroundings, from greys and browns to bright green. It camouflages well. There is a dark, lateral band bordered in white along the flanks, which varies in the different sub-species. In the typical form (*Hyla arborea arborea*) this extends from behind the eye to the groin, and curves in the lumbar region. Its distribution is western and central Europe from France and northern Spain to Germany and beyond to the Caucasus and Urals. Further sub-species occur farther south, in the Mediterranean region including the islands, and in the Canaries and Asia Minor.

It lives mainly in marshes, reedy beds of ponds and lakes, often in parks and gardens where there is access to water. It clings with its sucker-like finger and toe-pads to leaves, bark and walls. The breeding spell is short, during which it descends into water to spawn, then returns to the bushes and trees. At this time the male usually develops a bluish tinge on its throat. The throat-fold swells up to a large size, and vibrates as it

67

croaks loudly and rapidly, usually after rain or at night.
Vivarium: 6, 8, 9. A lofty vivarium is recommended in which
tall pot-plants and branches can be placed. Breeding is possible
if plenty of space is given. The author has had success by using
a greenhouse containing a grapevine and a water trough.
Escapes have settled among the rose bushes in the garden. Introduced colonies have existed in various parts of Britain from
time to time. Has been kept for fourteen years.

American Tree-frog (Hyla versicolor)
This familiar American species occurs in southern Canada, and
in the United States from Manitoba through Dakota, Kansas
and Oklahoma to the Gulf States. About the size of the European Tree-frog, it has a more toad-like shape, a more warty
skin, and conspicuous digital discs. Colour varies with its
surroundings, from pale-grey or green to brown and even black.
There is a darker, star-shaped patch on the back. It camouflages
well. General habits and breeding are similar to those of *Hyla
arborea*. The male gives a loud, resonant trill, frequently heard
as a background noise in jungle films set in totally foreign lands.
Has been kept for seven years.

Two further species of hylids are worth mentioning. The
Golden Tree-frog (*H. caerulea*), is Australian, and has an
attractive golden tint in its skin. It measures about 2in. Even
smaller is the little Spring Peeper (*H. crucifer*), which has a wide
distribution throughout North America. It is only about 1–1½in
long, and gives a high, whistle-like call, loud for its size.
Vivarium: as for *H. arborea*.

Marsupial Frog (Gastrotheca marsupiata)
This interesting species, a near-relative of the hylids, belongs
to a group of South American tree-frogs. Eggs are carried in
the back of the female, in a purse-like brood pouch which
opens by a narrow mouth to the rear. Breeding this species in
captivity has been successful in recent years, and the author
has witnessed the mating at one British zoo where the specimens
were kept in a tropical greenhouse, and given access to a water
trough. However, the metamorphosed young did not survive.

Page 69   (*above*) Grass Snake (*Natrix natrix*). The wide gape of its mouth as it swallows the frog is made possible by separation of the lower jaw-bones; (*below*) Anaconda or Water Boa (*Eunectes murinus*). This constrictor spends many hours submerged in the lakes and rivers of its native South America

Page 70   (*above*) European Tree Frog (*Hyla arborea*). The typical sub-species, *H. a. arborea*, shown here, reveals clearly the lumbar curve in the lateral band of colouring; (*below*) Clouded Iguana (*Cyclura carinata*). The larger iguana species are normally kept in zoos, but, with patient handling are tameable

Vivarium: 4, 8, suitably heated, and with access to water. Has been kept for five years.

Family Brevicepetidae—Narrow-mouthed Toads
This family of Narrow-mouthed or Pug-nosed Toads belongs to tropical lands. In Africa they are called Blaasops, meaning 'blow-up', from the way in which they swell up their bodies with air. The family consists of many small species, some only 1½in long. The majority have narrow pointed heads. Mostly they burrow and some climb. In some species, eggs are laid on land and develop directly into toadlets.

Cape Narrow-mouthed Toad (Breviceps gibbosus)
There are many 'pug-noses' to choose from, but this particular species is well-known and common in southern Africa. It has the typical characteristics of the family—a plump body covered by a warty skin, and a narrow pointed face. The dull colouring blends with the soil in which it burrows. It is essentially terrestrial, and lives on the veldt. Eggs are laid under a stone or log, and full metamorphosis through the tail and gill stages takes place within the egg-capsule. A baby toad eventually frees itself.
   Vivarium: 1A, 2, 3. Keep warm and give plenty of loose soil.

Family Pipidae—Tongueless Toads
This primitive group of toads (Aglossa) are placed in a single family, the Pipidae. They are tropical and entirely aquatic. There are no eyelids, and in other respects too they retain a few fish-like characteristics. Their interest to biologists has made them familiar to herpetologists and aquarium keepers. The few species are confined to South America and Africa, and they have been successfully bred in confinement.

African Clawed Toad (Xenopus laevis)
This is the best-known African species, and has become famous in medical circles as a pioneer subject for the human pregnancy test. Treated urine from a woman is injected into the toad; should she be pregnant then the hormone present will stimulate the toad to spawn.
   Xenopus can measure up to nearly 5in. The flattened body is

E   71

round and plump and has a smooth slimy skin which makes it almost impossible to hold. Head and eyes are small by comparison. There is no tongue or tympanum. Limbs are held out stiffly. The fore-limbs have pointed fingers and are used for detecting and pushing food into the mouth, the powerful and fully webbed hind-limbs have claws on the three outer toes of each foot, hence its name Greek, *Xenopus* = 'strange foot', Latin, *laevis* = smooth. It is known in Africa as the Platanna.

This lively swimmer can move with sudden bursts of speed, either forwards or backwards, and will dart to the surface for quick snatches of breath, then, just as quickly, submerge again. Colour is usually a mottled brown to grey, pale or dark according to surroundings. Its range extends from Abyssinia to the Cape, and it lives mostly in vleis, ditches, marshes and slow streams in the veldt country, and open grassland. During drought it buries into mud and aestivates. Breeding usually follows the rains. Food is searched for in the mud with the sensitive fingers, or caught at the surface.

Spawning occurs at various times according to the season, between June and September in the Cape area. Amplexus is around the groins and the male twitches his body to stimulate egg-laying. The pale eggs are laid singly among water plants. In the early stages the tadpoles hang in the water, head down, with a flickering motion of the tail. They have two antennae which are probably used as tactile organs. They are filter feeders of microscopic water life. Adults are voracious feeders and will tackle almost anything in the way of animal life they can catch. In the water, *Xenopus* can produce a curious ticking sound which sounds like the winding of a watch.

Vivarium: 5, suitably heated at 77–80° F. To stimulate breeding, allow some of the water to evaporate, add some water plants, then top up the aquarium with a watering can to simulate a rain shower. Mating may then follow. This is an easy and amusing species to keep and breed. Other, smaller, *Xenopus* species, such as *X. gilli* are also kept. It has a more spotted belly and is locally called the 'sago-tummy'. *X. laevis* has lived for fifteen years.

72

Surinam Toad (*Pipa americana*)

This New World cousin of the Clawed Toad is of equal interest and curiosity as an aquarium inmate. It occurs in swamps and slow-moving streams in Brazil and the former Guianas. It grows to about 4in, and the flattened, rounded body has a small, triangular head. There are short, tactile tentacles and skin flaps around the mouth. The fore-fingers have curious, star-shaped appendages which probably help in locating food. The skin, a dull brown to grey, is smooth and slippery.

Habits resemble those of *Xenopus* as far as swimming and feeding is concerned, but breeding is quite different. After the onset of rain a male grips a female in amplexus around the groins. When about to spawn she extrudes her oviduct about an inch, and this retroverts along her back. As the eggs emerge they are squeezed into the spongy tissue on her back by the male. A pouch forms around each egg with a kind of lid on top. On parting the female withdraws her oviduct. Eggs later hatch into larvae and remain in the pouches for about three to four months. At metamorphosis the young swim free.

Vivarium: 5. The same treatment as for *Xenopus*. Occasional success has been achieved in breeding—a fascinating thing to watch. Has lived for five years.

CHAPTER 6

Newts and Salamanders

In this order of amphibians, the Caudata, the tail is retained for life. The 150 or so species are found almost entirely in the northern hemisphere, the majority in North America. As with frogs and toads, some species are entirely terrestrial, others enter water to breed, and others are permanently aquatic.

Apart from a few live-bearing species, eggs are laid, either singly or in clumps, covered and protected by a jelly coating, and are usually attached to objects such as water plants, stones and tree roots. During breeding there is no amplexus, or at most only a clumsy attempt on the part of the male to grip the female. In some species, however, a form of courtship takes place; the male develops a courtship dress, and postures and dances before the female. This is especially the case among the so-called newts of the family Salamandridae. Having attracted a mate the aroused male deposits a small packet of sperms in a cluster called a spermatophore, which the female takes up by the lips of her cloaca. Sperms ascend the oviduct to fertilise the eggs. It is believed that the stimulus to this mating is provided by scent emitted from the glands of the male. This mating behaviour is typical of all tailed amphibians. The time of spawning depends on the latitude and altitude of the breeding area and can start as early as February, or as late as June.

The tadpoles differ from those of frogs and toads, in having more elongated bodies; also from the moment of hatching they feed on an animal diet of microscopic life.

Family Salamandridae
This family is spread over the northern hemisphere, and includes the many species, called newts, which live on land but enter the

74

water when they breed, among them the genus *Triturus*, of which there are three species native to Britain. The various members of the genus *Triturus* make interesting and attractive aquarium subjects during their breeding season. Their graceful swimming movements and courtship habits can be readily observed at close quarters. Maintenance of a healthy stock depends on regular feeding: a variety of small water creatures such as tadpoles and water fleas, as well as small earthworms and pieces of raw meat, may be used. When they are ready to leave the water after breeding, the newts should be transferred to a land vivarium, if they were being kept in an aquarium. The aqua-terrarium will serve as a home all the year round. The rearing of young is referred to on page 56.

Common or Smooth Newt (Triturus vulgaris)
This familiar newt has a range stretching from Britain across Europe as far as the Balkans and Urals, and from Scandinavia down to the southern Alps and Italy; it also occurs in Asia Minor. There are nine different sub-species. Habitat is almost any kind of terrain in the vicinity of ditches, pools, ponds, drowned pits and other still waters. It does, however, tend to avoid mountains and acid soils.

This species grows to about 4in and varies in colour from brown, more so in the female, to an olive-brown; with rows of darker spots, larger in the male. This pale-rose or yellow underside has a median area in orange or red, spotted in black. During courtship the male develops a wavy dorsal crest along the back and tail, the lower edge being orange with a blue border. Females are without any crest.

Courtship consists of a 'dance' performed by the male. He approaches a female and nuzzles her with his head, then throws himself into a stiff attitude on raised toes, and curls his tail in a bow. The tip then vibrates rapidly in the face of the female. On emergence after breeding the newts hide under stones and other cover, and are sometimes mistaken for lizards (which are reptiles and scaly). Hibernation can occur on land or under water.

75

Vivarium: 1A, 2, 3 (when on land) and 5 during breeding, 6 and 13 as permanent homes. Has been kept for eighteen years.

Great Crested or Warty Newt (*Triturus cristatus*)

This fairly large species grows to over 6in, the female can be even larger. The dark, almost black, body has a warty skin marked with darker spots, the flanks are stippled in white and the belly is yellow or orange with black spots. The male during breeding develops a high, serrated crest, separated from the tail crest by a sharp dip. There is a pearl-coloured stripe down each side.

Popularly called the Triton, after the Greek water-god, this newt extends over most of Europe north of the Alps, as far east as central Russia and Asia Minor. In Britain it is localised. General habits are similar to *T. vulgaris*, but it is more a lowland species of wooded country, and inclined to be more aquatic and to live in deeper water. Mountains are avoided.

Vivarium: see *T. vulgaris*. It requires deeper water for breeding. Has been kept for twenty-eight years.

Palmate Newt (*Triturus helveticus*)

This is a small species growing to about 3in .Colour is an olive-brown, usually paler in the female. It can be mistaken for a small Smooth Newt. Differences to note are the finer markings in the colour pattern, placed in more regular rows. The underside is more whitish with a median band of pale orange. The throat is a pale cream and, unlike in the Smooth Newt, rarely spotted. The male has a low, straight crest during breeding, and the tail ends abruptly in a fine thread. Hind toes are webbed in black.

Habits are similar to *T. vulgaris*, but it occurs more frequently on acid soils, in small pools and ditches, also in mountains. The range is over most of western Europe as far as central Germany, and includes Britain.

Vivarium: as for *T. vulgaris*. Has been kept for eighteen years.

Alpine Newt (*Triturus alpestris*)

This attractive European species is of average size, about 4in long. It extends across Europe, from eastern France to the Urals and Balkans. Colour in the male is grey to black, sometimes bluish, with sky-blue flanks speckled with black, and a clear yellow to orange belly. The male has a low crest, coloured yellow with a dark zig-zag band. Its name is misleading as it may occur in lowland pools as well as in mountains. Habits and breeding are similar to those of *T. vulgaris*.

Vivarium: see *T. vulgaris*. This newt can withstand low temperatures. Has been kept for fifteen years.

Marbled Newt (*Triturus marmoratus*)

This handsome species grows to much the same size as the Great Crested Newt. It is attractively coloured a bright to dark emerald green, marbled in black. The belly is grey to brown, spotted black and white. The wavy crest of the male has vertical bars in black, green and white. The female has an orange dorsal line.

Habitat is almost any stretch of stagnant water. Distribution is the Iberian peninsula and south-western France, where it takes over from *T. cristatus*. It has similar habits.

Vivarium: as for *T. cristatus*. Has been kept for eight years.

Spotted Newt (*Triturus viridescens*)

This is one of the best-known and most widespread of North American newts in this genus. It occurs over most of the eastern States, as far south as the Gulf States, and also around the Great Lakes. It inhabits pools, swamps and other stagnant waters, in woodland as well as open country.

Somewhat slimly built, it has a smooth skin and grows to about 3in. The breeding male has a low, straight-edged crest, which is also found in the female whose tail is much narrower and more depressed. Colour is olive-green, but can vary from yellow to a dark, greenish brown. The belly is yellower and the whole body is covered in small black spots. Along the back are two rows of red spots ringed in black.

Habits are broadly similar to those of the European species, except for a different kind of courtship. Adults enter water in spring, which can be as late as May or June in the north. The

77

male develops excrescences on its toes, feet and thighs, and attempts to clamber on to the back of the female, holding on with its hind-legs. In America, the immature young, at the stage when they leave the water to live on the land, are referred to as red-efts. This term is inspired by their reddish-brown colouring in the first year or so of life, which fades as they reach maturity.

Vivarium: as for *T. vulgaris*. Has been kept for five years.

Japanese Fire-bellied Newt (*Triturus* [*Cynops*] *pyrrhogaster*)

This eastern newt has now been placed in the same genus. It lives in the paddy fields along watercourses and drainage ditches in Japan, and grows to about 4in. Colour is some shade of deep-brown to olive; the belly is bright red, dotted with black. A lateral skinfold gives it a squarish appearance. Toes are long and pointed, so is the tail. There is no dorsal crest, but a prominent ridge along the backbone. Courtship is similar to that of *T. viridescens*, with the male attempting a clumsy pick-a-back on the female.

Vivarium: as for *T. vulgaris*. Has been kept for twenty-eight years.

Spanish or Ribbed Newt (*Pleurodeles waltl*)

This is the largest newt in Europe, and can grow up to 12in. It is found in the Iberian Peninsula and also in Morocco. The thickset body is covered in warts, with raised folds of skin along the sides. There is also a row of orange glands down each side, from which the tips of the ribs sometimes protrude, possibly as a protection against predators, as in the case of fish with spiny fins. The colour of the back is olive-grey to bottle-green, marked with dark, rounded spots; the underside is a greyish white and the lower edge of the tail orange. A breeding male has dark pads on the underside of the forearms.

This very aquatic species seldom leaves the water, and is somewhat sluggish in movement. It inhabits pools, marshes and muddy places, into which it will burrow during drought. Hibernation seems doubtful, except at high altitudes. Breeding is intermittent. The male crawls under his mate, and grips her in the armpits with upraised forearms. Eggs are laid singly or in clumps.

78

Vivarium: 5. Best kept isolated because of its size and appetite, otherwise treat as for the other newts. Has been kept for twenty years.

European or Fire Salamander (Salamandra salamandra)
This famous salamander, of the genus *Salamandra*, has an undeserved reputation for being deadly poisonous and able to withstand fire. The first part of this ancient legend, believed since medieval times, is possibly explained by the bitter-tasting fluid which can be secreted from the skin glands, and by the salamander's bright colouring, considered by naturalists to be an example of 'warning colouration' to deter predators—a kind of 'do not touch' because of the unpleasant consequences. Its supposed immunity to fire could be explained by the fact that, when a salamander hibernates, it might well hide away in a wood-pile. A log is placed on the fire one day, and a salamander crawls out; if the log is damp and puts the fire out, so much the better for the legend. Certainly few animals will molest it.

The body of this species is of robust build, with a broad head and rounded tail. There are vertical grooves along the sides of the body and on the tail. The smooth skin has many pores, especially on the prominent parotid glands, which secrete the 'poison'. There is no crest or webbing on the toes. Its vivid colouration consists of spots or stripes in black and yellow to orange. Average length is some 5in but specimens can reach 11in in southern Europe. Male and female look much alike, but can be distinguished by the more swollen cloacal region in the male.

The species is widespread, from the Atlantic coast to the Balkans and parts of Asia Minor and North Africa—ten subspecies in all. The two commonest are the Spotted Salamander (*S. s. salamandra*) of central Europe, which tends to be spotted, and the Striped Salamander (*S. s. terrestris*) of western Europe which tends to be striped. However, there are variations.

Mainly nocturnal, the salamander remains hidden by day, coming out after rain or at night. It is sluggish in movement, and when found cannot be mistaken. Habitat is damp and shady

79

surroundings, in woodland, among rocks, particularly in mountainous country.

Pairing may take place in almost any month, apart from the time of hibernation. A male will pursue a female, butting her in the flanks, then clamber on to her back, and hook his forearms around hers in a loose amplexus. A spermatophore is laid and picked up by the female, or it is transferred direct from his cloaca to hers. Gestation lasts for several months. The female then half enters shallow water, in a kind of hip-bath, and at intervals over several days produces gilled young. Up to seventy have been known. About three months later, the metamorphosed babies emerge as brightly coloured replicas of their parents. A female can retain the male's sperm and has been known to produce young in captivity, as late as two years after mating.

Vivarium: 1A, 2, 3, 6. This is a land species and only requires a shallow dish of water in case of breeding. The author's specimen, collected from the Harz mountains in Germany, has been kept for twenty-seven years.

Alpine Salamander (*Salamandra atra*)

As the name suggests, this is a montane species. It extends throughout the Alpine regions of Europe, also to mountains to the west side of the Balkans. It seldom lives below 2,600ft above sea level, and has been found as high as nearly 10,000ft, well above the timber line. It is entirely terrestrial, and hides under logs and between roots in woods, and under stones and moss in open ground. Average length is 4in. More slender than its spotted cousin, the European or Fire Salamander, it has a smooth, glossy black skin with vertical grooves along the sides and tail. The parotids are prominent as in *S. salamandra*, the male is distinguished by the more swollen cloacal region.

Much of its time is spent in hiding. Mating and birth of young take place on land, during mid-summer. A male climbs on to the back of a female, his forelimbs hooked under hers. The spermatophore is received in the usual manner. Gestation may take up to two years. The oviducts contain up to twenty eggs, but usually only twins are born, one to each oviduct. The other eggs break down into a fluid mass, which is absorbed as nourishment for the two successful embryos.

Vivarium: 1A, 2, 3. This is not a very successful captive at low, warm altitudes. It should be kept in cool surroundings, and allowed to hibernate.

Mountain salamanders (genus Euproctus)

The members of this European genus of three montane species live separately on the islands of Corsica and Sardinia, and in the Pyrenees. They are *Euproctus montanus, E. platycephalus* and *E. asper*, and may be encountered during mountaineering expeditions or ordinary holiday visits. All three are adapted to high altitudes, and can withstand low temperatures. The lungs are much reduced, and much of the oxygen intake is through the skin.

Drab in colour, in shades of grey or brown, the three species are slimly built, and about 4in long. Breeding takes place in mountain streams, usually between rocks. A male pushes his body beneath the female and twists his more strongly built tail around hers, in a grip from which she cannot free herself. This may last a day or so, when a spermatophore is passed directly between them. Eggs are attached to stones. Specimens found at low altitudes may be from larvae which have been washed down by the current.

Vivarium: 1A, 2, 3. These salamanders are not easy to keep and breed. They require cool surroundings with access to clear cold and, if possible, moving water. The author has not had much success. Little is known about their habits. They are a challenge for any vivarium keeper to tackle.

Family Ambystomidae—Blunt-nosed Salamanders

North America is the home of these salamanders. Like their European opposites they are mainly terrestrial, except for breeding, and pass through a gilled, larval stage. Some species of fairly widespread distribution are given here.

81

Spotted Salamander (Ambystoma maculatum)

This species occurs in the eastern states of America, around the Great Lakes, and southwards as far as Louisiana. It is stout bodied, about 6in long, with a slightly compressed tail. Colour is a deep, bluish-black; more slate-coloured on the sides and below. Along each side of the back is a row of yellow or orange spots. Habitat is mainly deciduous woods near pools and slow streams, but avoiding mountains. Adults migrate to water in spring, and there may be some lively courtship among the colony. Spermatophores are deposited, and females later lay clumps of spawn attached to submerged objects.

Marbled Salamander (Ambystoma opacum)

This is a small species compared with other salamanders—up to 4in long. The rather thickset body is attractively coloured a deep, lustrous black, contrasting with large transverse markings along the back which are white in males and greyish in females. This salamander migrates to water and breeds in autumn. Eggs are laid singly, here and there, under stones, behind bark, in moss and other hidden places. Such situations become flooded by late summer rains, the eggs can then hatch and the larvae swim away.

Jefferson's Salamander (Ambystoma jeffersonianum)

This is a slender species which grows to 6in. The elongated rounded body has a long and strongly compressed tail. It occurs around the Great Lakes and the north-eastern states. Colour is a uniform dark-brown, paler on the sides and below. Sexes look similar. Habitat is woodlands where there are swamps, pools or slow-moving streams. During breeding the male may embrace the female. Clumps of spawn are attached to underwater supports.

Tiger Salamander (Ambystoma tigrinum)

This most widely distributed member of the family extends across the States, from the Atlantic coast to the Rockies, and from southern Canada to the Mexican Gulf. It is the largest species, measuring up to 7in on average, but some males have reached

10in. There are five sub-species. The body is stout and muscular, and shows vertical folds along the sides. Ground colour is a deep-brown to black, covered in a scattering of pale-brown or yellow spots which are more or less strongly marked, according to the sub-species.

Essentially a burrowing salamander, it spends much of its time below ground. This may explain the wide variety of habitat it can live in, such as deciduous and coniferous woodland, open plains, mountains and even semi-desert. In spring a breeding pond is resorted to, and there is much sparring as male and female nose and push one another with their snouts. Clumps of spawn are later deposited by the female.

This species was once thought to be the adult stage of the famous Axolotl of Mexico (below), which is a separate species. *Vivaria:* The above ambystomid salamanders may be kept in the same way as their European cousins, but will require access to water if they are to breed. Some kind of home on the lines of an aqua-terrarium will enable them to enter water when need arises.

Axolotl (permanent larval stage of Siredon mexicanum)
Famous in research as a laboratory animal, also as an aquarium pet, the Axolotl (Aztec, *nahuatl* = water beast) is a true case of neoteny, in that, in its native habitat in the lakes around Mexico City, it retains the larval characters of gills and a swimming tail as a mature adult. This is thought to be due to a genetical defect which inhibits thyroid activity, possibly as the result of a selection process. These Mexican lakes, formerly in lush surroundings, would have been suitable for a metamorphosed larva to live as a land salamander. Today the locality is more a semi-desert, so that a permanent life in water is far safer. At any rate it is possible to transform the axolotl into an adult with thyroid treatment.

In 1865 specimens were sent to the Paris Natural History Museum, and began to breed. Of the ensuing larvae, one transformed into a land salamander, and left the water. This happened a number of times until breeding ceased. Some years later, when

83

specimens were transferred to new quarters, breeding recommenced.

Axolotls can grow up to 8in long, and are now bred in the albino form, as well as in the more natural dark-grey or brown marked with darker spots. A metamorphosed adult has the normal body shape of a land salamander, with a rounded tail, no crest and breathes with lungs. It is a dullish grey with yellow spotting.

At one time the Axolotl was thought to be the young of the American Tiger Salamander (*Ambystoma tigrinum*), but is now placed in a separate genus as the Mexican Salamander (*Siredon mexicanum*).

Vivarium: 5. An aquarium of well-matured water of at least 8in depth is required. The Axolotl does best in cool shady surroundings; it has survived in the author's garden the whole year round. To transform a specimen, thyroid treatment may be tried, but is best done under the supervision of an experienced doctor or veterinary surgeon. An easier way is to allow the water slowly to evaporate, meanwhile providing an island platform. The author has only had partial success, since the animals died before the gills had fully disappeared. Young specimens are advised for this experiment.

Family Plethodontidae—Lungless Salamanders
This family of small- to average-sized salamanders embraces the majority of the American tailed amphibians. Oxygen is taken in through the lining of the mouth. Living on land, the majority hide away in damp undergrowth and among rocks, in caves and in damp places in woodland and marsh. Some are brightly coloured in yellows and reds.

In Europe this family is represented by the genus *Hydromantes*, the Cave Salamanders which inhabit caves and rocky places in mountainous areas. They are found on Sardinia, in the maritime Alps and in northern Italy, but little is known of their habits.

Dusky Salamander (Desmograthus fuscus)
This common species is found throughout the eastern and Gulf states, in suitable localities. It inhabits woodland on the borders

of streams, also ditches and swampland, and is usually found under a log or stone, behind bark or debris. It is very terrestrial.

During courtship the male rubs his head against the female. The eggs are deposited in a small cluster beneath a log, stone or piece of bark, and attended by the mother. This repository is in the near vicinity of water—a female has been known to remove her eggs to a damper spot during a drought.

The larvae which hatch out wriggle their way into water, but not before they have developed their gills and swimming tails, which may take one or two weeks. This seems to be a curious reversal of the normal development of an amphibian, which commences life in water.

Yellow-spotted Salamander (*Ensatina croceater*)

This very attractive salamander is coloured a vivid black and orange. It is a mountain species, and is found along the foothills of the Rockies, from Canada to California, at elevations of about 5,000ft. Little is known of the breeding habits. This species is chosen as an alternative vivarium inmate to *Desmograthus fuscus* and as a challenge to further study.

Red Salamander (*Pseudotriton ruber*)

This is one species of a very attractive genus of North American salamanders which are brightly coloured in spotted reds and browns; the Red Salamander is coral-red. It extends through the eastern states, from New York to the Gulf, and lives in the usual damp situations such as damp meadows, woods, swamps and ravines, hiding under logs, stones and bark, usually close to water. Eggs are attached to submerged objects.

Red-back Salamander (*Plethodon cinereus*)

This species is completely terrestrial, and is commonly found hidden under logs, bark, in leaf-mould or moss, usually in wooded country. It occurs in the eastern states and around the Great Lakes. It has a slender build, and grows little more than 2½in. There are two colour forms: one is dark-grey to black with a broad band in yellow or bright red along the back; in the other, the band is more a lead-grey.

There is an extended breeding season during late summer and autumn, even as late as December. Eggs, resembling a miniature bunch of grapes, are laid in a cluster on a stalk and are commonly found inside rotten logs. Full development takes place within the eggs, which are attended by the mother; and the young only free themselves when they have lost their gills. They have been discovered on hatching as late as the following August. There is virtually no water stage.

Vivaria: 1A, 2, 3. These plethodontids live well in captivity, and do not require any standing water in which to breed, merely moist surroundings and hiding places. Their breeding habits are interesting to follow.

Family Proteidae
This family name is taken from the sea-god Proteus. These are permanently aquatic salamanders, and include the strange Olm or Proteus (*Proteus anguineus*) of south eastern Europe, which inhabits underground streams in limestone mountains from the eastern Alps, through the mountain ranges of Yugoslavia, into Dalmatia. It has been the subject of much close study, and is kept and bred inside cave laboratories in the Pyrenees. It lives in permanent darkness, at a constant low temperature of 5–10° F, is a dull white and has only rudimentary eyes. When exposed to light, pigment is formed and it darkens. Both egg-laying and live births have been observed.

This is a species best left to the experimental biologist. However, there is the following American species in the same family which does well in the aquarium.

Mud Puppy or Water Dog (Necturus maculosus)
This is a fairly large aquatic salamander which grows to about 12in. The robust body is coloured a rusty brown, with rounded, blue-black spots scattered over the back and sides. The bushy gills are red. This species inhabits a wide area of the eastern half of the United States. It lives in clear water in streams, lakes and canals, and may annoy fishermen by taking their bait. Sexes are similar, but the cloacal difference will help to identify.

Mating takes place in autumn, the female laying her eggs in

86

Page 87 Giant Zonure (*Cordylus giganteus*). With a spiny coat to help restrict water loss, Zonure lizards are well adapted to withstand arid conditions

Page 88   (*above*) Common Chameleon (*Chamaeleo chamaeleon*). A master of camouflage, this member of a curious Old World lizard family is easily overlooked; (*below*) Common Gecko (*Tarentola mauritanica*). This particular native of the Mediterranean was found under a stone on the island of Majorca

the following early summer, usually in some depression behind a stone or submerged log away from the water current. She usually remains in attendance.

Vivarium: 5. The size of the tank will depend on the size of the individual. A large bath, water-trough, etc could be modified; during summer a pond could even be used. Large salamanders like this one will take frogs, fish, crayfish and pieces of raw meat.

Family Sirenidae—Sirens

This is another aquatic family which have elongated eel-like bodies. Only forelimbs are present, and these much reduced. In North America, sirens occur mainly in Florida and in the coastal regions of the eastern and gulf states.

Great Siren or Mud-eel (*Siren lacertina*)

This is another aquatic salamander which can reach 3ft. It is coloured a pale grey, and has greenish gills. The tiny four-fingered forelimbs help it to hold on to underwater vegetation and objects. Sirens prefer weed-choked pools, ditches or marshes. Eggs are laid in clumps, but little appears to be known about the breeding habits. It has been kept for twenty-five years.

Vivarium: Depending upon size, a large tank, well filled with vegetation, is required. Feed as for Mud Puppy (above).

Family Amphiumidae

This is another American family of eel-like, aquatic salamanders, which possess front and rear limbs, but of minute size. The adults have lungs. The range is broadly similar to that of the sirens.

Two-toed Congo Eel (*Amphiuma means*)

Specimens up to 3ft have been reported. Shape, size and habits are generally similar to those of the Great Siren, but there is another sub-species which has three toes each limb. Eggs are laid in strings in some underwater burrow, and are attended by the mother. Although capable of breathing air, these amphibians to not leave water. A specimen has been kept for twenty-six years.

Family Cryptobranchidae—Giant Salamanders

This small family of only two species includes the world's largest salamander, the biggest of all Amphibia. Gills are missing in the adult, but there may be traces of gill slits.

Japanese Giant Salamander (Megalobatrachus japonicus)

This, the world's largest amphibian, has been known to reach a length of nearly 4ft. It lives in hill streams in Japan and China, and is sometimes caught for food. Some herpetologists recognise another, very close relative *Megalobatrachus maximus*, but this is in dispute. The Giant Salamander has a somewhat flattened body, with heavy skin-folds along the sides. The tail is webbed and the limbs short, stocky and broad. Colouring is some shade of grey to brown. Eggs are laid in strings, each attached to the other by a central cord. A specimen has been kept by the Amsterdam aquarium for fifty-two years.

Hellbender (Cryptobranchus alleganiensis)

This American species grows to about 2ft in the female, but smaller in the male. It is similar in build to the Japanese Giant Salamander. The soft body has wrinkled folds along the sides, and colour varies from a dull yellowish brown to black marked with darker spots. It occurs in the eastern United States, from the Great Lakes to Georgia and Louisiana, especially in the rivers which flow from the Allegheny Mountains.

During summer eggs are laid in two long strings, resembling rosary beads, and are attached in a tangled mass to some submerged object or depression. An unusual feature for salamanders is that fertilisation by the male is external. She spawns and he emits a cloud of milky, seminal fluid over the eggs. He will guard the nest with head facing the opening. In about eighteen months the larvae lose their gills, and are about 4in long.

Vivarium: (for large salamanders) members of the above two families (Amphiumidae and Cryptobranchidae) which grow to a large size, obviously need more space. If young specimens can be obtained so much the better. A large aquarium, water-trough or pond is suggested, bearing in mind that some members live in running water and breathe through gills. A Giant Salamander kept by the author, which was 3ft long, lived for some years in a large hip-bath.

This, and on other occasion a Mud Puppy and a Great Siren, were interesting enough as specimens for study, but rather disappointing as aquarium pets. Long intervals were spent in just doing nothing. At feeding time they would suddenly spring to life, in crocodile fashion, and snap at a meal. A warning: the bite of these animals can be severe and painful! Bathers in America are sometimes bitten.

CHAPTER 7

Lizards and Snakes

By far the majority of modern reptiles consist of lizards and snakes which belong to the order Squamata (Latin *squamus* = a scale). Lizards form the sub-order Sauria of about 3,000 species, and snakes of the sub-order Serpentes about 2,600 species. Both have a coating of overlapping scales, but otherwise appear to have little in common. The reason for grouping them together is a technical one. Fossil evidence, although meagre, suggests that they have a common ancestry, and shows close affinities in the way the skull is constructed. But, apart from some lizards which have elongated bodies and are limbless, and a few snakes which resemble lizards, the distinction between the sub-orders should be obvious. In general snakes are limbless and have no movable eyelids. Lizards (except geckos) can open and close their eyes. Many lizards fracture their tails whereas snakes do not. A snake's jaw-bones are loosely jointed and flexible, enabling it to swallow large meals (see page 118); lizards' jaws are more like ours, and only articulate where the lower jaw joins the skull.

An interesting feature in both groups is a sensitive pit in the roof of the mouth, called Jacobson's organ, which communicates through nerves to the brain. It is an aid to smell. Snakes and many lizards, in particular the monitors, catch particles of scent on the tongue and transfer this to Jacobson's organ. The flickering tongue is testing the air for signs of danger, or prey. This explains why a snake when alarmed or hungry will move its tongue more rapidly as it tests its surroundings.

Lizards can hear, and in many there is a visible ear-drum, or tympanum. Snakes are deaf in the accepted sense, and have no ear-drums. It is very doubtful whether they hear the sound of the snake-charmer's music. A rearing cobra is merely on the defensive, and sways its body in order to keep an eye on the musical instrument which the snake-charmer moves from side to side. On the other hand snakes are highly sensitive to ground vibrations. Even a footstep will send a snake into hiding, and could explain why so few people ever meet one.

LIZARDS

Sub-order Sauria Lizards are among the most numerous of reptiles and also the most versatile and diversified. They are adapted to all kinds of living: for swimming, climbing, burrowing and even air gliding. They range world-wide, and live below ground, on the surface, or in bushes and trees, in habitats ranging from swamps to deserts. Food in the main consists of insects and other invertebrates, although larger species can tackle small mammals and birds. A few are vegetarian.

Family Lacertidae—Typical Lizards
To herpetologists in Britain and Europe this is the best-known family, and consists of some 150 species. Small to medium-sized, these lacertids have elongated and conical shaped bodies, well developed limbs and tail, and a conspicuous tympanum. There are no adornments such as frills and throat-fans or spines. Many males colour up during the breeding season. Except for the Common or Viviparous Lizard (*Lacerta vivipara*), all are oviparous. These Old World lizards are found throughout Eurasia and Africa, and some have become established in America. Mostly they prefer dry situations, and spend long intervals sunbathing. In Europe they are a common sight among ruins visited by tourists. The genus *Lacerta* is probably the best-known group of lacertids, either encountered in the wild or offered by the pet trade.

Common or Viviparous Lizard (*Lacerta vivipara*)
This is the only ovo-viviparous species of the genus, and has a very wide range, both in latitude and altitude. It extends from

93

the Atlantic coast right across Eurasia to the Sakhalin Islands, north of Japan, and from the Alps and Himalayas to well within the Arctic Circle. In Britain it is the only reptile found in Ireland. The length with undamaged tail is about 6in. Colour varies and can be grey, brown, reddish or greenish, usually with a dark stripe along the back. The dark band along each side is speckled orange in the male, more yellow in the female. Occasional melanic specimens turn up. The male's belly is a spotted vermilion or orange. This hardy little lizard turns up in colonies in many undisturbed places, usually those on the dry side and where the sun reaches, such as heaths, woodland glades, hedgerows, waste ground, cliffs and mountain slopes, up to quite high altitudes. Young are born in late summer, almost black in colour.

Vivarium: 1B, 2, 3, 9, 12. Fairly dry conditions are advised, with access to sunlight if possible, also a water-dish for drinking. Although a live-bearer, this lizard has been known to lay eggs at high altitudes. The author has experienced this by keeping a gravid female in damp, cool and dim surroundings, away from sunlight. The mother produced young still inside the egg-sac and containing yolk. They did not survive. Has been kept for six years.

Sand Lizard (*Lacerta agilis*)

Despite its descriptive name this species is not particularly active. About 8in total length, it has a rather stoutly built body and blunt snout. Its distribution is western Europe, from the Channel coast across to west Russia, and from Scandinavia south to the Alps, Balkans and Caucasus. It is very localised in Britain, in danger of extinction, and best left alone. Specimens are common enough on the continent. Its habitat is dry and sandy areas, such as sand-dunes and heath land which is not too overgrown, also steppe country in eastern Europe. Colour, somewhat variable, is grey, brown, even reddish, with sides and underparts bright green in the male during the breeding season. The female is paler, more greyish. Along back and sides are dark bands with 'eye-spots' of deep brown with white centres. A bright-coloured male could be mistaken for a Green Lizard (*Lacerta viridis*). Habits are generally similar to those of *L. vivipara*. Eggs are laid in a shallow hole dug beneath some cover.

Vivarium: as for *L. vivipara*. Provide a good layer of loose soil mixed with sand and peat. Has been kept for six years.

Green Lizard (*Lacerta viridis*)
This handsome species grows to about 15½in. The colour is grass- to yellow-green in both sexes. The male has a thicker head and broader base to its tail, and turns sky-blue on the throat during the breeding season. It extends across central and southern Europe, from northern Spain, through southern France, Italy, parts of Germany, the Balkans and south-west Russia. Habitat is dry localities among rocks and on waste land, in sunken lanes with bank sides, and in conifer woods. It is shy and agile, and a good climber. The female lays up to twenty eggs. It hunts insects, also small mammals and birds, and eats occasional fruit.

Vivarium: as for *L. vivipara*. Give plenty of sunshine. Has been kept for ten years.

Eyed or Ocellated Lizard (*Lacerta lepida*)
This is Europe's largest lacertid, and it can grow to more than 23in. Fine and colourful, it has a strong, thickset body. The cheeks are swollen and the tail long. Colour varies from brownish-green to reddish, covered on the back in a close network of dark lines, sometimes forming into rosettes with black centres. The flanks are ocellated with blue patches ringed in black. The range is Spain, Portugal and southern France. It lives mainly on the ground, among rocks, on hillsides sometimes at high altitudes, and in woodlands. Because of its size it will catch other lizards, small mammals and birds, apart from various insects. The bite is powerful but not dangerous.

Vivarium: as for *L. vivipara*. A fairly roomy cage is needed. Has been kept for nineteen years.

Wall Lizard (*Lacerta muralis*)
This very abundant European lizard has a widespread distribution, and has been divided into as many as fourteen sub-species.

An average length is 8in. The body is slender and the head narrow and tapering. The typical sub-species (*L. muralis muralis*) range throughout central and southern Europe, from Holland, Belgium and France to Germany and Poland, and southward to the southern mountain ranges. The other sub-species exist in various parts of the Mediterranean region, including the islands. Dry and rocky terrain, in sunny places where it can bask, is preferred. It turns up in ruins, vineyards, among rocks and walls, and in gardens and town parks, and is a familiar sight to tourists. Colour is variable in some shade of grey to brown. White or greenish bands, sometimes broken into spots, run along each flank, the upper band passing along the tail. The belly is white, yellow or orange. Has been kept for five years.

Vivarium: see Ruin Lizard (*L. sicula*).

Ruin Lizard (Lacerta sicula)
This species has even more forms than the Wall Lizard. It is the largest and most attractive of the so-called wall lizards, and can grow to nearly 10in. Its main range is in Italy and Sicily. The general build is similar to that of *L. muralis*. Colour is brownish to grey, with a bright, blue-grey back marked in longitudinal rows of dark spots.

Vivarium: as for *L. vivipara*. Plenty of sunshine is recommended, with bark and rocks to rest on and hide under. The last two species and a number of others, loosely called wall lizards, inhabit most of the Mediterranean area, including the islands. The Bibliography should be consulted for more details as to identity and distribution. There are some thirty species to choose from.

Sand Racer (Psammodromus hispanicus)
This species inhabits Spain and southern France, and has a close relative, *Psammodromus algerus*, which extends into north Africa. They grow to about 10in and are covered in a rough skin because of the strongly keeled scales. The slim body is light-brown to olive, and has a pale stripe along each flank. Habitat is sandy and rocky places, in scrubland.

Vivarium: 1B, 2, 4. Some heating is required. Give plenty of sand.

Keeled Lizard (Algyroides fitzingeri)
An average length for this lizard is 4½in. It has a similar build
to the Sand Racer, but has extra-large, overlapping, keeled
scales on its back. It lives on Corsica and Sardinia. Colour is a
plain olive-brown, with a pearl-grey throat and bluish snout.
Belly and legs are yellow. A further species (*Algyroides nigropunctatus*) belongs to south-east Europe—Yugoslavia, Albania
and the Ionian Islands. It measures 8in. Colour is brown to
olive-green, shading off to black, and speckled with dark spots.
The lower sides and belly are brick-red in the male, more
greenish in the female, and it has a blue throat.
   Vivarium: as for *Psammodromus* (immediately above).

Family Gekkonidae—Geckos
This is a very distinctive family of lizards, adapted for climbing.
The special features are the large, ever-open eyes with vertical
slits, and the pads on the fingers and toes which give a firm grip
on vertical surfaces, even when upside-down. The structure of
the toes is used in classification. Mostly tropical and nocturnal
geckos hide away by day or cling to bark and walls against
which they camouflage well. They are a familiar sight, and
sound, in dwellings, and in many cases are encouraged to live
there in order to control the insects. They can become very vocal
when calling or disputing their territory, and emit a variety of
chirps, clicks, squeaks and barks. The tail is fragile and easily
breaks. Geckos are oviparous, and normally lay two or three
eggs at a time, which take many months to hatch.

Common or Wall Gecko (Tarentola mauritanica)
This is the familiar gecko of the coastal areas of the Mediterranean. It occurs from Spain to Greece, along the north-
African coast to Egypt, Israel, Syria and the Ionian Islands. Its
large and flattish body is covered with flat scales interspersed
with keeled tubercles, in longitudinal rows. Colour varies from
grey and brown to almost black. Length is about 4½in. The toes
are uniformly flat, and have a single row of broad lamellae
underneath. Third and fourth fingers and toes have claws. It

frequents rocky places and walls in low-lying country, often entering gardens and outhouses, and can move at high speed. When alarmed it emits a high squeak. Hibernation is doubtful, but it will retire during cold weather. The female lays a pair of eggs in late spring or summer, and incubation lasts for about four months. It occasionally appears in daytime, to lie and bask in the sun.

Vivarium: 1B, 2, 3, 4, 8. Since these lizards climb, a tall vivarium containing branches, bark and tall pot-plants is advised. Water is drunk from rain or dew on the leaves, so these should be sprayed occasionally. Has been kept for seven years.

Naked-fingered Gecko (*Gymnodactylus kotschyi*)

This smaller species grows to about 4in. It is more slimly built, and has narrow fingers and toes, swollen into a pad at the base, each having a single row of lamellae. Colour is pale-grey to dark-brown. It occurs in southern Italy, Greece, the Balkans, as far as Bulgaria and the Aegean Islands. It inhabits rocky places, usually hidden by day under stones and between cracks.

Leaf-fingered Gecko (*Phyllodactylus europaeus*)

This is an example of a third type of gecko, whose fingers and toes widen out at the tips. Underneath are two rows of lamellae with a groove in between, into which the claws can be withdrawn. It grows to 2¾in. Colour is a light or dark greenish-yellow, marked with darker bands and black spots. The tail is constricted at its base.

House Gecko (*Hemidactylus frenatus*)

Known by this rather vague common name, the House or Half-toed Gecko represents a large tropical genus of average size. Specimens occur in Africa and the Far East, and are widely known in dwellings. One or two species have been introduced into the West Indies by shipping. Each toe ends in a sharp claw with an expanding pad behind. The two rows of lamellae are covered in fine, hair-like projections, which enable it to cling on to a rough surface in any position. The popular belief that geckos can actually stick on to something by suction is untrue; rarely can a gecko cling to a smooth surface, such as polished wood or glass. This species is the familiar *chee-chak*, to give it the Malayan name, to be seen scampering over walls and on ceilings in many homes.

Great House Gecko or Tokay (*Gekko gekko*)

Named after its sharp, barking cry, this is one of the largest geckos, up to nearly 12in long in some cases. It inhabits southeast Asia, Malaya and the Indonesian islands. Many a newcomer to these parts has been startled by the sudden, loud alarm cry of 'to-kay' in his bedroom or bathroom, or even in a restaurant or hotel lounge. Dwellings are its favourite abode, where it is welcomed as an insect catcher. The Tokay is coloured grey, and is covered in orange and red spots.

Vivaria: see *Tarantola mauritanica*. Most geckos can be kept in such surroundings, but provided with warmth, especially if tropical. Be careful to avoid any escapes. The author has spent many hours searching for, and chasing after, these lively lizards. Be careful in handling, since the tail can be fragile.

Family Chamaeleontidae—Chameleons

Of all living lizards the chameleon is the most bizarre. Known widely for its colour changes, it has many other peculiarities. Most specimens are arboreal and slow-moving, and must rely on their camouflage, not only to escape the eyes of an enemy, but also to approach within striking distance of a meal. The illusion is so good that one might say a chameleon not only looks like a leaf but behaves like one. The body is thin when facing, and leaf-shaped when side-on. Since the tail is prehensile this could be mistaken for the leaf-stalk. In movement the chameleon sways its body backwards and forwards with each slow foot-step, as a leaf might move in the wind. The five toes are united into two opposing bunches, and give a firm grip on a branch.

Colour change has been the object of much study and observation. Pigment cells in the skin react to various stimuli and are controlled by the nervous system. The different coloured granules, such as black, white, brown, etc change position and inter-

99

act to give a range of colours which usually blend with the surroundings, but not always so. Temperature, light intensity, even emotions, play a part.

Chameleons tend to be rather solitary and quarrelsome lizards, defending the territory in which they live; a stranger entering a bush or tree may be driven off by the occupant. The author once witnessed such a display of emotion almost equivalent to human stress. A strange specimen was placed in a cage occupied by a chameleon. The resident reared up, puffed up its body with air, opened its mouth, hissed and went 'black with rage'. The newcomer shrank down on the branch, went 'white with fear', and fell off! One minute a chameleon may be a pale spotted grey, and the next a vivid green with heavy barring.

The chameleon's remarkable bulging eyes are almost wholly covered by lids, leaving only a tiny peep-hole, and they can swivel in any direction. Each works independently. The animal can be looking forward with one eye at some insect prey, and over its shoulder at an enemy with the other. However, when about to catch food both eyes swivel forward and, by moving closer, a careful judgement is made so that the long tongue will reach its target. This is club-shaped at the end, and sticky. It rarely misses as it shoots forward.

True chameleons are entirely Old World. The so-called American 'chameleon' is quite different (see page 112). Some half of the eighty species occur in Africa south of the Sahara, the other half in Madagascar. Two species occur in Arabia, one in India, and another just inside Europe along the Mediterranean.

Size varies from about 4in to giants as much as 2ft long. Some species, mostly males, have adornments such as helmets, or casques, over the neck; others possess horns. Among the really large species, four are worthy of mention: *Chamaeleo oweni*, found in the African rain forests, and Jackson's Chameleon (*Ch. jacksoni*) which is more a species of open, bush country. Both have three horns and are reminiscent of some prehistoric dinosaur, such as the *Triceratops*, in miniature. Indeed, they have been used in movies to represent these prehistoric giants.

100

Meller's Chameleon (*Ch. melleri*) another large African species, is known to catch birds. The fourth, *Ch. isabellinii*, has a single horn.

Chameleons are mainly oviparous, and come to the ground to dig a hole and bury their eggs. Some, found in southern Africa, produce young, and usually live in cool surroundings in mountains. These small, ovo-viviparous chameleons do not need to leave the bushes and trees, since their young are born above ground and can cling on to the branches as soon as they are born.

Common Chameleon (Chamaeleo chamaeleon)
This is the Mediterranean species, found in the coastal areas, from Spain across northern Africa to Israel, Arabia, Syria and parts of south-west Asia, as well as on some Mediterranean islands such as Crete and Cyprus. Total length is about 10in. The casque on the head is shaped like a kind of triangular helmet. The back is ridged with a row of scales like the teeth of a saw. The tail is prehensile. It lives in bushes and trees, especially in olive groves. About twenty eggs are laid in the ground.

Flap-necked Chameleon (Chamaeleo dilepis)
This is an African species found in eastern and southern Africa. It grows to about 13½in. There is a well-developed movable casque behind the head. Up to thirty-five eggs may be laid.

Dwarf Chameleon (Microsaurus pumilis)
This common species is best known in South Africa. Young are born within the egg-membrane and become attached to branches by a sticky secretion which prevents a fall. The adults grow to about 3in. They often appear in gardens. Some ten or so young are born in one litter.
Vivaria: 8. A tall and roomy cage is necessary to accommodate these interesting pets, depending on their size. A good supply of branches, and some tall pot plants for cover are required, also a liberal depth of loose soil in which, with luck, eggs may be laid. The plants should be sprayed from time to time, and

the chameleon will lick them when thirsty. Since chameleons live among bushes and trees, only moderate lighting is needed, but warmth is necessary.

The author's experience with these fascinating lizards is limited, and no breeding has ever taken place under his care. However, one or two points can be mentioned. On the whole, unless they are a pair, chameleons live best on their own. As great a variety of food as possible should be offered, and the animal handled as little as possible. The author was fortunate in obtaining locusts as food for a Flap-necked Chameleon (*Ch. dilepis*). During one summer it lived in an isolated tree in the garden, with a circular disc of metal-sheeting fixed around the trunk to prevent it from wandering. It proved a popular attraction with visitors, but was sometimes difficult to detect among the leaves, so had a red ribbon tied around its tail!

Chameleons can prove disappointing captives, and do not seem to live more than a year or two.

Family Agamidae—Agamas
This family of some 300 species is entirely Old World, and mainly tropical. The handsome East Indian Water Lizard (*Hydrosaurus amboinensis*) up to 3ft long, is the largest. Many agamids are adapted to dry country in semi-desert and steppes, others prefer forests and are arboreal. Some burrow. Most agamids have cylindrical bodies with short, broad heads. During courtship there may be a good deal of competition between the males, even to the extent of biting one another. Courting is accompanied by much head bobbing, and a successful male grips his mate in the mouth during mating. Agamids are oviparous. A few examples are given here.

Sling-tailed Agama or Hardun (*Agama stellio*)
This is a semi-desert species widely distributed over Egypt, the Middle East and some Grecian islands. It grows to about 12in. The body is covered from head to tail in sharply pointed scales. The colour varies from yellow to brown. A row of pale-yellow patches runs along the back and tail. Warm and dry surroundings, where it lives between rocks and ruins, are preferred. When

102

alerted it bobs its head up and down—a common sight in the Nile delta.

Spiny-tailed Agama (Uromastix acanthinurus)
This is another semi-desert species found in north Africa. It is even more spiny than *Agama stellio*, especially on the tail. This makes it look dangerous but belies a docile nature. It feeds on plants. Each individual has its own burrow, to which it retires when disturbed. Diving into a hole, it uses its tail to block the entrance. Spiny-tails are vegetarians.

Blood-sucker (Calotes versicolor)
This is a species of India and the Far East. The normal colouring is brown to olive-grey, marked with irregular dark spots and bars. When under stress or emotion during combat, a victorious male turns a reddish-brown. The Blood-sucker is an active climber and can grow to well over a foot long. It hunts insects and other small invertebrates.

Rock Agama or Koggelmannetje (Agama atra)
This agamid is a common sight in South Africa, being one of a number of species which inhabit the open veldt and mountain sides, in dry surroundings. It is usually noticed sitting on a rock in hot sunshine, bobbing its head in typical agamid fashion. Colour varies considerably according to background and emotion, from pale grey to almost black. The head may turn a bright blue. Females are less coloured. When disturbed it moves at high speed, even raised on its hind-legs and running two-footed.

Moloch or Thorny Devil (Moloch horridus)
This most grotesque lizard is covered with sharp spines rising out of conical swellings from head to tail. Two of these sprout from the head. Length is about 8in and the general colouring is a mixture of brown and orange, which blends well with the sandy areas in which it lives. This is an Australian lizard, perfectly harmless, which fact belies its name. Slow and deliberate in movement, it searches around for its diet of insects and termites. It is one of several species of agamid lizards which

103

could become the pride of a herpetologist's collection, and which may occasionally turn up in zoos.

Even more remarkable is the little Flying Dragon (*Draco*), of which a number of species live in the tropical forests of the Far East, from Burma southward to Malaya, Indonesia and the Phillipines. The ribs extend out of the sides of the body and support a membrane which can be spread out in wing-like fashion, so that the little creature can glide a considerable distance from branch to branch. The body colour is forest-green, but, as it springs into flight, the brilliant, orange wings, spotted with black, give it the appearance of a giant butterfly.

Australia and New Guinea is the home of the spectacular Frilled Lizard (*Chlamydosaurus kingi*). A scaly membrane resembling a ruff surrounds the throat. In face of danger this frill is raised and the mouth opened. The inside is a bright yellow or orange. At speed it can run fast on its hind-legs. Its close cousin, the Bearded Lizard (*Amphibolurus barbatus*), resembles it. When teased it turns from a normal olive-brown to a bright orange. The large Water Lizard, mentioned on page 102, has a large tail fin which is used when swimming.

Vivaria: 3, 4. Most agamid lizards should be given a cage containing sand or loose soil, with rocks to sit on or to lie under. Branches are required for arboreal species. The cage dimensions will depend on the size of the specimens, and food will vary according to the species.

Family Cordylidae—Girdle-tailed Lizards or Zonures

Equally adjusted to warm and dry surroundings are these Old World lizards. Southern Africa is their main domain. To withstand the intense heat and dryness of the veldt and desert habitat they have developed a strong coating of spines, especially on the tail. This is encircled with whorls of keeled scales and so also serves as a protection. To escape an enemy a zonure will wedge itself in between rocks from which it is difficult to dislodge it.

Giant Zonure or Lord Derby Lizard (*Cordylus giganteus*)
This is the largest member of this family, and grows to 14in.

It is spread widely throughout Africa, from Ethiopia to Cape Province. Its method of defence is to lie flat along the ground, limbs pressed against its sides, leaving its hard spiny back exposed to the enemy. It hunts small animals, and, when at rest, will sit motionless for long periods, staring into the sky. It is locally called the sonkijker or sun-gazer.

Armadillo Lizard (*Cordylus cataphractus*)
This zonure earns its name from a useful defence mechanism—the habit of grasping its tail in its mouth when attacked. In this coiled-up position it protects its soft belly. The battery of spiny scales is strengthened by a bony central layer which makes the lizard's surface as hard as stone, and almost impossible to bite into.
Vivaria: 3, 4. Zonures require warmth and sunlight, and can be treated like the agamids of similar dry and sandy habitats.

Family Skincidae—Skinks
This is primarily an Old World family of some 600 species. In many places they are the most abundant lizards, yet are seldom seen because much of their time is spent below ground or buried in leaf mould. Some inhabit desert country and others belong to forests. In a typical skink the body is slender and conical with a pointed head and tail, and is covered in small, smooth and shiny scales. Limbs are short, much reduced, or even absent. Skinks move in serpentine glides and can wriggle into holes, sand and undergrowth to escape an enemy. They readily loose their tails if grasped. Length varies from one or two inches to that of the largest species, the Giant Skink of the Solomons, which is more than 2ft long. One unusual feature is the 'window' —the lower eyelid is replaced by a transparent plate which covers the eye when closed, but allows for vision. This protects the eye when burrowing. Colour is mainly a shade of brown with longitudinal stripes and spots.

There is a tropical genus of skinks, *Mabuya*, which inhabit the forest regions of Africa, south-east Asia, Indonesia, Mexico and tropical South America. One species, *M. mabuya*, is a familiar sight in built-up areas in Brazil.

Common Skink or Seps (Scincus officinalis)
This is a common species which inhabits dry and sandy areas around the Sahara and Red Sea coast. It grows 8in, and has a stout and slightly flattened body covered in small rounded scales. The head is short and pointed. Colour is yellow to brownish, with darker brown bands across the body. Each scale has a small white spot. It basks a good deal, and will rapidly burrow into the sand if alarmed. The word 'seps', of Greek origin, means 'of evil repute' and refers to an ancient belief that this and similar skinks are highly poisonous. They are all quite harmless.

Ocellated Skink (Chalcides ocellatus)
Members of this genus are also of north African origin. This species occurs in Algeria, Egypt, Arabia, parts of the Middle East, Greece and on some islands in the Mediterranean. It has the typical slender body and tapering tail, with short legs. Some species have much reduced limbs, even down to mere stumps. This skink has a grey-green to yellow-brown body covered by a fairly regular pattern of small black patches with white centres. It may turn up in built-up areas, on rubbish tips and on waste ground, hidden under stones and logs.

Five-lined Skink (Eumeces fasciatus)
This is one of some twenty species of American skinks in this genus. They occur mainly in eastern parts of the USA, ie the states of Dakota, Oklahoma and Texas, across to the Atlantic seaboard. It lives in rocky wooded areas, in moist surroundings. The chocolate-brown body has longitudinal yellow stripes. The male's head turns blue during the breeding season. Length is about 9½in, tail is long, and limbs are well developed. The mother has been observed to 'brood' her ten or so eggs, by curling round them and even turning them at intervals.

Blue-tongued Skink (Tiliqua scincoides)
This Australian skink is ovo-viviparous, and produces a litter of about ten young. It can grow to about 12in. Limbs are weakly developed. The dark purple-brown body is faintly ringed in

yellow. Apart from the usual small animals, it will also feed on fruit, leaves and fungi.

Stump-tailed Skink or Shingleback (Tiliqua rugosus)
This is another Australian skink of about equal size. It has a thick-set body with a stumpy tail, and is covered in large rough scales resembling the surface of a closed-up fir cone. It lives in the outback and often gets trapped in wire fences. The female produces two offspring at a time, each half as long as the mother. Colour is brownish, with spots or irregular transverse bands in yellow.

Vivaria: 1A, 2, 3. Give plenty of loose soil, preferably sand, in which to burrow, with stones, pieces of bark, etc, under which to retire, but check first to see that the specimen is a sand dweller. Forest skinks need moister surroundings. As show specimens, skinks are disappointing, since they keep so much out of sight. Bright light or direct sunshine may encourage them to expose themselves.

Family Anguidae—Slow-worms
The popular name for this family is based on the European slow-worm (*Anguis fragilis*), which is also found in Britain. Needless to say, it is not a worm; neither is it blind as implied in its other name of Blind-worm. Actually the family varies widely in shape, and some New World anguids have a more lizard-like build with limbs. Unlike snakes, these have movable eyelids. Some are oviparous, others produce young.

Slow-worm or Blind-worm (Anguis fragilis)
This species of lizard shows the extreme specialisation towards a snake-like build. The elongated body is entirely covered in small, uniform, tight-fitting scales, each containing a bony centre, called an osteoderm. Colour varies from grey to brown, sometimes it is more reddish or even black. Darker stripes may occur along the body, especially in the female. Some specimens, usually males, have bright blue spots scattered over the body, giving rise to the name Blue-spotted Slow-worms. Total length with undamaged tail (which is frequently broken and regrown

107

as a stump) is about 16in. Habitat is almost any undisturbed place where its favourite food, such as slugs and other slow-moving invertebrates, is available. Colonies may be discovered on rubbish tips, along railway cuttings, disused earthworks, country churchyards, hillsides and the borders of woodlands. It hides under logs and stones and among trees, and occurs on lowland sites as well as on mountains. Distribution is over much of Europe from the Atlantic coast, including Britain, across to the Caucasus, Urals and Asia Minor, and from the Arctic Circle to the Mediterranean. Up to twenty young are born in late summer, and are easily recognised by the striking contrast between the bright silvery body and the dark stripe along the back.

Vivarium: 1B, 2, 3. It might be described as the ideal children's pet. It is harmless and easy to keep and feed, and will take slugs and small earthworms. Gentle handling is required, since the tail easily fractures (hence *fragilis*). Has been kept for fifty-four years; the author's specimen for ten.

Glass-snake or Scheltopusik (*Ophisaurus apodus*)

This is the only genus of anguids found in both hemispheres, in Africa, Asia, Europe and America. *Ophisaurus apodus* is the largest species, up to 3ft or more in length, and occurs in the Balkans, Caucasus, Asia Minor and south-west Asia. The body is long and snake-like, about the girth of a man's wrist, and has a deep furrow along each side. Colour is chocolate-brown or copper, devoid of markings in older specimens. Some five to seven eggs are laid. The young are ashen-grey on top, white below, with a dark stripe on each side of the head. The Scheltopusik's size and powerful jaws enable it to tackle lizards, mice and nestlings, apart from smaller invertebrates. It can crush a snail with its jaws.

There are three species of Glass-snakes in America, the best known being *O. ventralis* which occurs on the Atlantic coastal plains. It seems to prefer damp woodlands and meadows, and is sometimes turned up by the plough.

Vivarium: as for *Anguis fragilis*, given larger surroundings.

Alligator Lizard (Gerrhonotus coeruleus)
This genus is exclusive to America, and mostly distributed along the Pacific side, from British Columbia southwards to Texas and Panama. Unlike other anguids it has well-developed limbs with a long, slender tail on a skink-like body. Length on average is about 10in. The scales lie in regular rows along the body. Most specimens are dull coloured, in greys and browns. In Mexico they tend to be much greener, and have orange eyelids. The above species is found in California and Oregon, and northwards to British Columbia. It prefers the cooler, more humid areas, usually in conifer woods. It is oviparous and lays about five eggs. A more southerly species *Gerrhonotus multi-carinatus* is a live-bearer. These lizards easily fracture their tails, as one way of avoiding capture. Another is to void an offensive fluid, or to grasp the tail in the mouth to make swallowing difficult.

Vivarium: as for *Anguis fragilis*. Add a branch or two, since these lizards can climb.

Family Amphisbaenidae—Worm Lizards
These strange vertebrates are a herpetological puzzle. Called, for want of a better name, Worm Lizards, they are still not clearly placed in the animal kingdom. They resemble large earthworms, having long cylindrical bodies ringed with shallow grooves, no limbs, and no readily visible ears or eyes. They are almost completely subterranean. Movement over the ground is in a straight line.

Mainly found in tropical rain-forests of America and Africa, the hundred or so species grow to about 12in. Their blunt tails resemble the small head, and may have given rise to the belief in a two-headed snake. They are immune to the attacks of the ants and termites on which they feed, and use their nests as an incubator for their eggs.

There is one American genus *Bipes*, which has two minute forelimbs just behind the head, often mistaken for ears. It occurs in California and Mexico, as the so-called Florida Worm Lizard (*Rhineura floridana*). It looks and behaves in an earth-
109

worm-like fashion, and when disturbed will retreat into its burrow backwards, like its namesake. *Amphisbaena* means 'going both ways'. This animal, about which little is known, is mentioned as a curiosity and as a subject for further study.

Two species of amphisbaenids occur in southern Europe. *Blanus cinereus* is found in the Iberian peninsula, Morocco and Algeria, and *B. strauchi* in Asia Minor. Colour in both varies from yellow to pink. The body has the usual vertical grooves. These lizards turn up in dry and stony places, burrowing in the soil and under stones; they are often discovered in gardens.

Vivarium: 1B, 2, 3, 4. Give a good layer of loose and dry soil, with flat stones for cover. Warmth may be required during winter. Although seldom seen above ground, these lizards are worthy of further study as to their habits and breeding, about which little is known.

Family Teiidae—Teeid Lizards or Tegus

As in the case of iguanids, this family is characteristic of the New World, and none are found outside the western hemisphere. They form the counterpart of the Old World Lacertidae which, in many ways, they resemble. Some 200 species are known and confined mostly to the warm lands of Central and South America. Only one genus, *Cnemidophorus*, the race-runners, is found in the United States; it also extends southwards into Brazil. The whole family is very varied in size and habits, from a few inches long to a giant like the Caiman Lizard (*Dracaena guianensis*), which grows up to 4ft. Teeids are found in forest and desert, seashore and mountain. Many are burrowers.

Six-lined Racerunner (Cnemidophorus sexlineatus)

This is probably the best-known species of race-runners, so-named because of their active movements. This is a resident of fields, roadsides and open places, in dry and sandy areas. It lives mostly in low-lying country or hills, but not in mountains. It tends to live in colonies, and its general behaviour might be likened to that of the European Sand Lizard (*Lacerta agilis*), page 94. General pattern is six, well-defined, narrow, pale-blue to yellow stripes along the body to the base of the tail, with dark-

110

brown to black in between. Length is about 7in. When approached a race-runner lives up to its name by darting rapidly into cover. Up to six eggs are laid under some cover such as a stone or log.

Vivarium: 1B, 2, 3, as for European lacertids, in fairly dry conditions.

Two further and more spectacular teeids, both for size and appearance, are the above-mentioned Caiman Lizard (*Dracaena guianensis*), and the Tegu of Brazil and Colombia (*Tupinambis nigropunctatus*). The former inhabits coastal swamps, and has a flattened tail with a double crest for swimming. The giant Tegu is a ground dweller with a reputation for stealing chicks and eggs, and is locally named the 'poulterer's thief'. Its body is dark in colour, spotted and ringed with yellow. These two occasionally turn up in reptile houses.

Family Iguanidae—Iguanas

This large and varied family is the equivalent of the Old World agamids. Except for a few on Madagascar and the Fijis the 700 or so species are American. It is interesting that the two families never overlap, the one family taking the place of the other. This kind of convergence among different animal groups is accentuated by the close resemblance between some iguanids and agamas (see page 102).

One difference between them is the teeth. Agamids have permanent teeth, whereas iguanids lose them and have replacements. Should a tooth or two be found in the vivarium there is no cause for concern.

Some iguanas have laterally compressed bodies and are tree-climbers; others with more flattened bodies are ground lizards. Size varies from a few inches to giant iguanas up to 4ft long. The iguana's tail, usually long, is used in many ways—as a balancer, in swimming and climbing, and for defence. Like some agamids, they bob their heads up and down during courtship or when alarmed. Mostly they are oviparous, and some are vegetarian.

Species include the small and colourful anoles, the curious

111

horned lizards, fleet-footed fence lizards and giant iguanas. One genus, on the Galapagos Islands, is marine.

Common Iguana (*Iguana iguana*)
This large species and its relatives are often seen in reptile houses. They come from the forests of Central America, where they are often caught for their skins and for human food. *Iguana iguana* can grow up to 4ft long. Colour varies from pale to dark green, marked with darker cross-bands. The thickset body is covered in tubercular scales and there is a frilled crest along the back, also on the hanging throat-fold; this can be blown up when alarmed or during courtship. The powerful tail is a useful defence. When necessary this iguana can climb. Powerful limbs with claws are used for digging. Small animals of all description are caught and eaten.

Vivarium: as a vivarium pet this impressive lizard needs a roomy cage with warmth. When tame it becomes quite docile.

Carolina Anole (*Anolis caroliniensis*)
This average-sized iguanid belongs to a genus of mainly arboreal lizards which, like geckos, can cling to all kinds of surfaces. On the last-but-one joint of each toe are broad scales which give a firm grip. Many have signalling devices, such as a crest and a throat-pouch, which the males use for challenging rivals in territorial disputes. The 165 or so species, a quarter of the total Iguana family, range from Carolina through Central America to Brazil, and are common in the West Indies.

Anoles are oviparous, and usually live in loose colonies. The above species occurs in Carolina and Florida, and westward through the Gulf States to the Rio Grande. It is a familiar sight, and known as the American 'chameleon'. It changes colour readily, and almost puts a real Old World chameleon to shame. From a pale-brown or grey it can darken to almost black, turn green with all kinds of dots and streaks which come and go according to the temperature, light or darkness, and mood. When inflated the male's throat-pouch is a brilliant red. Adults are about 7in long and have a body flattened sideways, a long tail, and a head with a wedge-shaped, pointed snout.

112

This anole is commonly found in trees, shrubs, among garden plants and along bushes and fences. It avoids the open and stays more in shady and moist localities. During breeding in April to May the males establish their territories. There is much head bobbing and throat inflation, and the back fan is raised. They pursue the females, even to leaping from one branch to the next, and can readily escape from danger by taking to the water. A female usually lays two eggs, buried in loose soil or debris.

Vivarium: 3, 8, giving plenty of space with branches and leafy plants to live among. Anoles are popular pets in the United States. A sunny situation should be chosen for part of the day and a shallow bowl of water always made available, since these lizards soon die of thirst. Spraying the leaves is useful, as they lap up rain or dew-drops in the wild. A regular and varied diet of insects, etc, should be offered. Much of interest can be watched and studied with a small collection of anoles. Unfortunately their lives are short, not much longer than two or three years. In America, they are sometimes given the run of a screened verandah or sunroom, or even live freely around the house and in the garden, as geckos do in the Far East.

Great Basin Chuckwalla (*Sauromalus obesus*)

Seven species of this genus of iguanids are confined to the south-west United States and Mexico. They inhabit desert country as ground dwellers, and hide among rocks, also burrowing to a limited extent. They are of average size and feed on plants. *Sauromalus obesus* is a common sight in desert country, and lives among rocks, on barren ground and lava beds, mainly in California, Utah and Arizona. The somewhat flattened body and tail is covered in small, flat scales, and there are a number of skin-folds, especially around the neck. Normally seen basking on a rock, this wary lizard rapidly darts into hiding. It will swell up its body in between the cracks and is difficult to dislodge. It can detect danger several hundred feet away. Some five or six eggs are laid in rock crevices. Food consists of the more tender parts of desert plants.

Vivarium: 1A, 2, 3, 4. Plenty of sand and rockwork should be installed, as well as warmth, and it should be given as much sunshine as possible. The Chuckwalla does well in captivity and soon tames. Has been kept for eight years.

Fence Lizard (*Sceloporus undulatus*)

This widespread genus of active lizards occurs in arid parts of the United States, from British Columbia and New York State southwards to Panama. The average length is $2\frac{1}{2}$–3in. The oval-shaped body has a long, slender tail of about equal length. The skin is covered in rough, keeled scales, with a granular fold around the throat. The colour is a mixture of browns and greys, with darker markings. This is an efficient camouflage, making these lizards difficult to detect. The males have brilliant throat-patches of green and blue.

Fence Lizards live in varied habitats, some among grass or rocks as ground dwellers, others in trees. They range from lowlands to mountains. Some lay eggs and others are ovo-viviparous. The above species may be taken as an example of the genus. It is the most widespread, and is found in dry situations, on prairie land, among rocks, on hillsides and in conifer woods, ranging from New York to Mexico. It lays eggs.

Vivarium: as for the Chuckwalla. Feed on insects.

Texas Horned Lizard (*Phrynosoma cornutum*)

As with the Australian Moloch, which is an agamid (see page 103), this unmistakable American iguanid has a covering of very sharp, spiny scales. Its rounded, short-tailed and toad-like body is flattened. On top of the head and on the sides are sharp horn-like spines. There are six species of horned 'toads' as they are sometimes called, and they inhabit the dry desert areas of the south-western United States.

This particular species, which is the one most commonly kept in the vivarium, belongs to the Great Plains, also the desert country of Texas and Arizona. The body is about 4in long, rounded and flattened, with a sharp tapering tail. Colour varies from pale yellow or brown to a deeper, reddish-brown. It darkens, as many lizards do, with a fall in temperature, or with increased light. Behind the head is a dark, white-edged

114

patch, and a series of similar, rounded spots along each side of the mid-dorsal white line. The habitat is dry, flat country, among rocks and sand, into which the lizard can burrow. This is done with sideways rocking movement as it wriggles into the soil. Such behaviour makes it almost invisible, and is a protection from the sun. Up to thirty eggs are laid in the ground. A curious habit when handled or alarmed is the emission of drops of blood which are squirted from the eyes. The reason for this is obscure, but may be a way of discouraging an enemy, since the emission is an eye irritant. This lizard is quite harmless.

Vivarium: as for the Chuckwalla, in warm surroundings, but it can be allowed to hibernate. Feed on various insects and other small invertebrates; large quantities of ants are eaten in the wild. Has been kept for ten years. More has probably been investigated and written about this species than about any other American lizard.

Family Varanidae—Monitors

This is an Old World family of some twenty-three species of lizard within the single genus *Varanus*. Its members have the longest known history of any modern family, and go back to the dinosaur age. The family includes the world's largest lizard, the Komodo Monitor (*V. komodoensis*) familiarly known as the 'Dragon', and could well be mistaken for this mythical beast. In size up to 10ft long, and weighing a good 300lb, its shape, claws and long forked tongue only require the addition of fiery breath to become a dragon's living image. Earliest records of dragons stem from ancient China, where the creature was wingless and looked upon with benevolence. It hovered over the emperor's palace as a celestial guardian, so different from the western monster slain by St George.

Given strict protection by the Indonesian government, the Komodo Monitor lives in solitary state on the islands of Komodo and Rintja, where it was first discovered by a Dutch officer in 1910. Two specimens kept in the London Zoo became so tame that they could be handled. After death, a cast of one specimen was put on display in the Natural History Museum in London.

115

Monitors are mostly large tropical lizards, of slim but powerful build, on average about 6ft long. The smallest species is the Australian *V. brevicaudata*, only 8in long. Some species are good swimmers and have a tail flattened sideways. In some there is a sharp ridge along the top of the tail which makes it a formidable defence weapon which can inflict a painful blow.

Monitors hunt small animals according to size. In a snake-like fashion the long, forked tongue is in constant use, testing the air for scent by way of Jacobson's organ (page 92). Food is usually swallowed whole. Occasionally domestic animals such as chickens are poached; in return monitors are killed by humans for food and for their skins. Also, monitors will raid crocodile nests for their eggs. Movement on land is reminiscent of a crocodile. The body is dragged over the ground in a serpentine fashion but, during bursts of speed, a monitor raises itself on its legs.

Some confusion may arise with common names. In Australia monitors are called goannas, a corruption of iguana, which is mainly an American family (see page 111). *Varanus* comes from the Arabic, *ouaran* = warning. At a sign of danger a monitor will dash away, and often dive into the water, alerting all the neighbourhood.

Eggs are laid in decaying vegetation, or in termites' nests.

Vivarium: A large heated cage with bare boards is the best home, since any soil or plants are bound to be disturbed. The more aquatic species will require a water-trough. In the vivarium hobby, young specimens are usually kept, and will readily tame. Large specimens are normally confined to reptile houses.

A few examples are the Nile Monitor (*V. niloticus*), of Africa and the Malayan Monitor (*V. salvator*), which are physically equipped for digging, climbing and swimming. The Australian Lace Monitor (*V. varius*), belongs to the outback and is an expert tree climber. It usually ends up that way when hunted by the ranchers with dogs. The Indian Monitor (*V. bengalensis*), is more a jungle dweller.

Sub-order Serpentes or Ophidia In a hobby such as vivarium keeping there is much of interest to experience, and indeed much yet to be found out about amphibians and reptiles. Furthermore, a great deal of misconception and unnecessary fear can be overcome by a closer contact with them, no more so than by keeping a snake as a pet. Such fascinating, and indeed, beautiful, animals have distinct advantages over many other pets. If properly kept they seldom fall ill. There is no fur or feather to harbour parasites, and the scaly skin is dry and glossy to the touch. They are silent and peaceful in motion, and require little exercise. Once tamed they take readily to handling. Feeding is not a daily affair, and meals can be restricted to once a week, or even less often. However, two important points ought to be borne in mind. The main reasons for ailments are improper feeding and unsuitable surroundings. It is wise to ascertain before acquiring a snake what its natural diet consists of, and whether this is readily available. Secondly, the cage or vivarium should be kept on the dry side. A constantly wetted skin can lead to trouble when sloughing (see page 46).

Snakes number about 2,300 species, ranging in size from one or two inches to 30ft giants such as the South American Anaconda, and the Reticulated Python of the Far East. Despite an absence of limbs, snakes between them can crawl, climb, burrow, swim, and in some cases even glide through the air. Normal movement is in a serpentine glide. The body is curled into sideways loops (never up and down) in an eel-like fashion, and presses against projections over which it travels, so propelling the body forward.

Some more heavy bodied species, such as vipers and constrictors, can also move in a so-called rectilinear fashion, in a straight line. Muscles attached to the ribs and body wall expand and constrict in a wavelike motion along the body causing the skin to move as well. The broad belly scales (scutes) overlap along the rear edge and can slip forward without hindrance. On the return stroke they catch on to the surface of the ground, or a branch, and so push the snake forwards. In a sense it rows itself along the ground. In a confined space such as a hole, the body is pressed against the sides in loops, and the snake hitches itself along in a kind of concertina movement. Another, rather special kind of movement, called 'side-winding', is used by some vipers which live in deserts. The snake tends to move sideways, and seems to flow over the loose sand as it coils its body into a succession of loops.

Prey is some animal or other, which is caught and eaten whole. It may be swallowed alive, or first killed by a venomous bite, or constricted. Both upper and lower jaw-bones are loosely hinged and can be adjusted during swallowing. The tips of the lower jaw separate, and by a chewing action, each half is hitched forward over the prey by means of the sharp, backwardly curved teeth. To assist breathing, the windpipe is sometimes projected out of the side of the mouth. This is a slow and deliberate feeding process, almost painful to watch, and may distress some people. It is best that they do not keep a snake. Most snakes will take freshly killed food, once they become tame.

Family Boidae—Pythons and Boas

Undoubtedly these are the most spectacular serpents, and popular in zoos, circus shows and private collections. Once tamed they become very docile. A main problem is feeding, and finding space in which to keep one—a matter of cost and convenience. Usually young specimens up to about 6ft are kept as house pets, and can be suitably fed on rats, mice and small birds.

Pythons are the Old World counterpart of the American boas, and together are considered to be the most primitive of modern snakes. A curious relic from their four-footed ancestry, is the vestige of hind limb-girdles, composed of three small elements of the pelvis. Attached to this externally, on each side of the cloaca, is a horny claw, small in the female and much larger in the male. The latter uses them to grip his mate during pairing. Whereas boas are live-bearers, pythons are oviparous. Some female pythons will encircle their clutch, coil around the eggs in the simple nest, and twitch the body. The body tem-

118

perature of the mother rises during this incubation, which is unusual for a so-called 'cold-blooded' animal.

Prey is caught by stealth or concealment. Their attractive colour patterns blend with the surroundings, and a python or boa will lie motionless along a branch or by a watercourse. As prey comes within reach, the head darts forward to catch the victim, which is then quickly gripped in the coils. The ensuing pressure arrests breathing and stops the heart-beat. The prey is then swallowed whole. Normally shy of man, these constrictors will nevertheless lash out if approached too closely, and have been known on rare occasions to kill and even swallow a human, usually a child. As with some of the larger lizards, these snakes are caught for their skins. The following pythons are some of the better-known species usually kept in zoos or as pets. They occur in Africa, India, south China, southwards through Malaysia to Indonesia.

Indian Python (Python molurus)
This is one of the most widely kept large constrictors, and prized as a zoo and show specimen. It has a good reputation for docility, especially the pale-colour variety (*Python molurus molurus*), which is found in India. The larger and darker *P. m. buvittatus* inhabits Burma, Indonesia and Ceylon. It is more stockily built than the Reticulated Python and can grow to 20ft and weigh up to 200lb. Colour is a shade of brown with dark, irregular patches on the back, and rough circles along the sides. It is the stock-in-trade of the snake-charmer and showman, and makes compelling viewing when wrapped around a pretty girl. It has been kept for thirty-four years in the Philadelphia Zoo.

Malay or Reticulated Python (Python reticulatus)
This giant occurs in eastern Asia, Indonesia and the Philippines. It inhabits the denser forest zones, and can become unpopular as a thief of domestic animals such as fowls, cats, dogs and even pigs. It has been recorded up to 28ft long, and weighing up to 250lb. It can lay up to a hundred eggs, and has been kept for twenty-one years.

119

African Python (Python sebae)
The home of this species is south of the Sahara. It can exceed
20ft and tends to avoid humans. It is shy and sensitive, and in
the author's opinion does not tame so easily as the Indian
species, and will bite more readily. Bites from these constrictors,
although non-venomous, can involve severe laceration from the
sharp teeth.

Ball or Royal Python (Python regius)
By contrast this very handsome python is usually docile and
readily tames. Unfortunately it spends much of the time curled
up in a tight ball, and can make a disappointing pet. By gently
handling, the author managed to get a young specimen to stop
this habit. This python occurs in western Africa, from Nigeria
to Liberia. It can grow to 6ft.

Australian Python (Morelia argus)
This species, formerly *Python spilotes*, but now placed in a
separate genus, occurs in Australia and New Guinea. It climbs
freely, and has a long prehensile tail. It can grow to 12ft. Small
birds and mammals, especially rabbits, are hunted. Australians
call it the Carpet Snake or Diamond-back. Normally this
constrictor has the typical python colouring of dark markings
on a paler light-brown background. However, some varieties are
more bluish-black, with bright yellow spots on each scale and
yellow diamond-shaped marks along the back. Specimens are
encouraged to live on farms in order to keep down rodents.

Anaconda or Water Boa (Eunectes murinus)
The length of this giant has been reliably reported to be as much
as 25ft. Higher figures in news items are either false or exaggerated. It inhabits the Orinoco basin, the Amazon and the
former Guianas, spending much of the time close to, or in the
water. It will catch waterside birds and mammals that come
down to drink, even small caimans. The colour is a dark olive-
green, with darker, oval patches along the back, and dark rings
along each side. Families of up to thirty young are produced,
measuring about 2ft 6in.

Boa Constrictor (Constrictor constrictor)
In spite of popular belief this is by no means the largest snake, and seldom reaches more than 10ft. It occurs in Mexico, through Central America into South America as far as Paraguay and northern Argentina. It is attractively coloured a reddish-brown, with darker triangular markings having yellow centres and outlines situated along the back.

Rainbow Boa (Epicrates cenchris) and Emerald Boa (Boa canina)
These are two very handsome and prized collector's items. The former is a golden brown marked with dark, circular rings; the latter is a vivid green with a white criss-cross pattern along the back. Both climb well, especially the latter which is well camouflaged against the leaves. It has a very prehensile tail which can firmly grip a branch when resting or dealing with its prey. An average adult length in both species is 6ft.

Rosy Boa (Lichanura roseofusca)
This belongs to California and western Arizona. Little more than 3ft long, it lives in the chaparral country. It is slow-moving and seldom bites, but may roll into a ball if disturbed. Colour is an attractive pinkish-brown. Europe's only boa is the Sand Boa (*Eryx jaculus*), which grows to about 2ft 9in and is coloured pale-grey to yellow, with dark cross-bars along the back and spots along the sides. It occurs in Greece, the Balkans, Bulgaria and Asia Minor. It lives in sandy places and can burrow rapidly into the soil. Slightly larger is its cousin the Giant Sand Boa (*Eryx tataricus*), up to 3ft 4in long, which inhabits more the forest areas and steppe country. The range is the Caucasus across to the Urals.

Vivaria: a suitable home for a python or boa will depend on its size and habits. A special cage may have to be constructed for a large specimen, preferably out of wood. For small specimens up to 3 or 4ft which are those more usually kept, a showcase as used in shop displays would be sufficient. Branches will be required for arboreal species. Burrowers and sand-dwellers require a liberal supply of sand or loose soil, kept dry. Some

H   121

place of retirement is also necessary, such as a wooden box with a small aperture to provide a dark retreat, a hollow log, or a 'cave' of rocks. A water-bowl must be available at all times, also a larger container for the more aquatic species. Sunlight is not essential, since many constrictors live in a world of perpetual gloom. Heating not lower than 70° F should be maintained. Make certain that the cage or vivarium is escape-proof, so as to avoid alarm and resentment among the neighbours, also embarrassment to the owner. Situations like this usually end up in the popular press, and are sometimes exaggerated. The author makes it a rule to see that all cages are padlocked.

Family Colubridae—Typical Snakes

This very large family consists mainly of harmless species. Although wild-caught specimens may bite when first handled, and cause a lacerated wound with their teeth, only a few are capable of producing venom which can be serious. Mostly they swallow prey alive, and some constrict as the big snakes do.

The non-venomous kinds, such as the Grass Snake (*Natrix natrix*), belong to a subdivision called the Aglypha, and those which can inject poison belong to the Opisthoglypha. Their fangs are situated at the back of the jaw, and the venom is rather weak. They are not considered really dangerous to man, since the fangs do not usually reach the hand which is bitten. However there is one potentially dangerous opisthoglyph, the African Boomslang (*Dispholidus typus*), an active tree-snake which has caused fatalities. Normally good-tempered it will bite on provocation. These back-fanged species are usually tree-dwellers, with slender bodies; some can launch themselves from tree to tree, and glide through the air.

Although this book is not concerned with the venomous snakes, mention should be made of the two families of venomous species, in case they should ever be encountered in the field. One of these, the Elaphidae, consists of the cobras, kraits, mambas, coral snakes and sea snakes. Sometimes called the Proteroglypha, they possess fangs which are fixed in the front of the upper jaw. When approached a cobra will rear up, and in

122

some species spread its hood in an aggressive fashion, then lunge forwards to strike. It hangs on and chews at its victim in a somewhat clumsy fashion, so that the venom flows into the wound. Far more efficient is the biting mechanism of the members of the family Viperidae. Here the fangs are fixed to movable jaw-bones which can be raised and lowered when required. The body is coiled so that the head can be launched at high speed when the viper strikes. Venom is injected through hollow fangs, and operates with the efficiency of a doctor's hypodermic. Not a drop is wasted. The true vipers, mainly Old World, and the Pit-vipers, such as the American rattlesnakes, must always be treated with respect. However, it should be emphasised that, with rare exceptions, no snake will deliberately attack.

Grass or Ringed Snake (Natrix natrix)
This genus of harmless snakes, sometimes called water snake (Latin *nato* = to swim), are popular as pets, and the above species is commonly kept by British school-children. It occurs widely over England and Wales, but not in Scotland. There are no snakes in Ireland. In Europe it extends from the Atlantic coast to the Danube delta, the Caucasus and Asia Minor, and from Denmark to Italy and Spain. Nine sub-species are recognised, that in Britain being called the Barred Grass Snake (*Natrix natrix helvetica*).

The typical sub-species (*N. n. natrix*) of central and southern Europe is coloured grey to brown, olive-brown, occasionally black, and is marked with rows of dark markings along the sides and back. Behind the head are two moon-shaped, yellow patches, bordered behind in black. The barred sub-species occurs in western Europe, from Britain to the Rhineland, south to the Pyrenees and Alps, and gets its name from the rows of narrow, vertical bars along each side of the body. The moon patches are usually yellow to orange. The general colouring is grey, brown or reddish, with an olive tinge.

Average size in Britain is between 2 and 3ft, longer in females, but can reach 6ft in southern Europe. It tends to inhabit areas in the vicinity of water, at sea-level or in mountains, up to

123

6,500ft. It is an expert swimmer and hunts frogs, toads, newts, fish and occasional small mammals and nestlings.

Although harmless it will hiss and dart its head about when handled, but never seems to bite. A further defence is the voiding of an evil-smelling fluid from the anal glands. It will also sham dead by turning over on to its back, with mouth wide open. These reactions soon cease once the snake is tamed.

Eggs up to thirty are laid among rotting vegetation, in manure heaps and fermenting haystacks, or wherever warmth is available.

Vivarium: 1B, 2, 9. A drinking-bowl should always be available and, if possible, access to sunlight. This temperate species can be hibernated. Has been kept for nine years; in the author's case, for six years.

Dice or Tesselated Snake (*Natrix tesselata*)

The range of this species is broadly similar to that of the Grass Snake but extends further east into Russia, across Asia Minor and into western China and India. It can grow to 4ft. Colour is grey to olive-brown, marked with a mosaic pattern of squarish patches along the back and sides. The head has an indistinct V-mark. This is very much an aquatic snake, spending long intervals in water with the head just showing. Food is similar to that of the Grass Snake, fish being especially liked. Habits are similar.

Vivarium: as for Grass Snake. Provide an ample water-dish.

Viperine Snake (*Natrix maura*)

The common name of this snake indicates its resemblance to an adder. On a green-grey, reddish or yellow-brown background there is a dark, wavy or zig-zag pattern running along the back. Along either side is a row of eye-spots with white centres. It ranges through southern Europe from the Iberian peninsula and France through north-west Africa, the islands of Corsica and Sardinia, and parts of Italy. It prefers similar habitats to the Smooth Snake (page 126) and feeds on similar prey. Adult length is up to 4ft. It swims well and tames readily.

Vivarium: as for the Tesselated Snake (immediately above). Food is similar.

124

Common Water Snake (Natrix sipedon)
Like its European relatives, this American species usually turns
up in areas of wetland, where there are suitable retreats such as
low vegetation, ditches, tree-roots and other hiding places. It
occurs through most of the north-eastern states, and hardly a
pond, swamp or stream is without its quota of water snakes. It
grows to about 3ft and is coloured dark-grey to dark-brown,
with indistinct pale cross-bands along the body. Many are
killed in mistake for the venomous water moccasin, a pit-viper,
which can be recognised by the white colour of its mouth when
opened, hence the other name for it of Cottonmouth. Unlike
the European species, the American Water Snake produces
young.

Vivarium: 1B, 2, 3 as for Grass Snake, given an ample water
dish.

Hog-nosed Snake (Heterodon contortrix)
This interesting American snake has much in common with the
European Grass Snake, in particular its behaviour when
molested. Although quite harmless it will put up a fine display
of bluffing, swelling up its body, and rearing up with flattened
head and neck in a cobra-like fashion. If this fails to intimidate
it performs the 'death' trance. Locally it is called the 'puff-
adder' or 'sand-viper'. Adult length is about 3ft.

It is named after the sharply keeled, upturned scales at the
end of its snout. This is a useful tool when burrowing into the
soil. The somewhat thickset body is coloured a deep olive-blue,
pale yellow underneath. This is accentuated by the bright
colours revealed between the scales when the body swells up.

It inhabits open woodland, farmland and beaches, usually in
sandy places and lives on a diet strictly of toads, rather than
the usual variety of food taken by small snakes. The three
species cover the Atlantic States and the western Plains. Up
to twenty-five eggs are laid.

Vivarium: 1B, 2, 3 as for the Grass Snake.

Smooth Snake (Coronella austraica)

This species is so-named because its scales have no keels, thus giving the skin a smooth feel. It occurs over much of western and central Europe, from south Sweden and Norway to northern Spain and Portugal, Italy and Greece. A close relative, *Coronella girondica* occurs more to the south, in the Iberian peninsula, Italy and Greece. In Britain the Smooth Snake has always been confined to the heathland and dry open woodlands of southern England, mainly in the Hampshire Basin, and is becoming rare. Its habitat is similar to that of the equally rare British Sand Lizard (*Lacerta agilis*, page 94) and it is seldom seen. It should be left alone. Specimens are common on the continent, where it lives mostly on heaths and dry woods, from sea-level up to 6,500ft.

It is a small snake, seldom more than 2ft long. Colour is reddish-brown or greyish, with darker markings in transverse rows or spots across the back, and a dark stripe through each eye and on the head. It is ovo-viviparous. Food consists of small mammals, and especially lizards—the old name for it is the Lizard Snake. Prey is held in its coils to restrict movement while the snake swallows. Although quite harmless it is inclined to bite when first handled.

Vivarium: the Smooth Snake makes a docile and attractive pet, and lives well in captivity. Provide the vivarium with sand and dry vegetation such as heather, also a water-bowl in which it will lie on occasions. A German specimen kept by the author lived for ten years.

Common Garter Snake (Thamnophis sirtalis)

The genus *Thamnophis* is the most widespread of North American snakes, extending from Labrador to Mexico and the Gulf States. It is the popular schoolboy pet in the USA. Similar to the European Grass Snake, it has a slender body and broadly similar habits, such as a fondness for water, the same defence mechanism of producing a foul-smelling fluid, and a fondness for cold-blooded prey. In addition, earthworms are eaten. A difference is that Garter Snakes are ovo-viviparous, and can

126

produce large families of up to seventy or so young.

The above species ranges from the Atlantic seaboard inland to Minnesota, Missouri and Texas, and from Nova Scotia, Quebec and Ontario south to the Gulf of Mexico. It grows to about 3ft. The slender body is coloured dark-brown to olive-grey, occasionally greenish, and has a yellowish band along the back, and one along each side covering the second and third rows of scales. A very similar species, called the Ribbon Snake (*Thamnophis ordinatus*), has the lateral bands on the third and fourth rows of scales.

These snakes prefer moist open places, in meadows, woods, marshes and along ditches and field borders. They commonly turn up in parks and on rubbish tips, even inside large towns. Apart from being live-bearers, their habits are similar to those of the European Grass Snake.

Vivarium: as for Grass Snake. This popular North American snake tames readily, is harmless and easy to keep, and usually gives no trouble with feeding. Has been kept for six years.

Racers or Whip-snakes (*Coluber*)

Racers or Whip-snakes of the genus *Coluber* are widely kept in the vivarium, and make handsome pets. Their slender lithe bodies and speed in movement have earned for them these popular names. They are among the fastest moving snakes, and speeds of up to 4 or 5mph have been recorded. This may sound disappointing in view of some of the sensational stories about their powers of locomotion, but it is the rapid twisting of the body and the quick disappearance into cover, which creates an illusion of high speed.

These colubrids are somewhat aggressive when first handled, inclined to bite, and not always easy to tame. Patience and careful handling may be required. They are mostly hunters of small mammals, birds, and even other snakes. In many parts of the States they are encouraged to live on farms, in order to keep down the rodents. They occur in North America, Mexico, Europe, north Africa and Asia. Prey is not constricted, as in the case of the genera *Elaphe*, *Lampropeltis* and *Pituophis* (see

127

below). Many species reach a length of 6ft or more, and all are ovi-parous.

Dark Green or Angry Snake (Coluber viridi-flavus) This is the largest European species, reaching a length of 6ft or more. It occurs on the southern Alps, in Italy, the Balkans and some Mediterranean islands. Colour is a deep-green or brown, with yellow spots in transverse rows on the front part of the body, which form into longitudinal rows towards the tail. Each scale has a yellow spot. It occupies the drier woodlands, rocky areas and is found between low bushes in vineyards and seldom enters water. It is inclined to be aggressive.

Horseshoe Snake (Coluber hippocrepis) This is another south-European species, inhabiting the Iberian peninsula and north-west Africa. Colour is mainly a dark, reddish-brown, marked with a chain-pattern of white. Behind the head is a horseshoe-shaped dark marking, with the open ends pointed backwards. It inhabits dry and rocky mountain slopes.

Blue Racer or Black Snake (Coluber constrictor) This species belongs to the mid-western and eastern states of America, from Maine to Florida, and across to the Great Lakes and the Mississippi. It has an immaculate black colour which reflects a bluish tinge. The habitat is woodland clearings, open fields, hedge-rows and farmland. In spite of the scientific name it does not constrict, but holds down its prey under the weight of its own body. *Vivaria:* as for King snakes (page 132).

Climbing Constrictors (Elaphe)
Of the colubrids, only the *Elaphe* and *Lampropeltis* species tend to kill their prey by constriction, as the big snakes do. The *Elaphe* genus occurs in America, Europe and Asia, and, like the *Lampropeltis* genus, has a number of common names. Snakes of these two genera are known as King, Corn, Rat and Chicken Snakes. Their general diet consists of small mammals, birds and other snakes. Most are capable of climbing, and can cling to branches. Some are beautifully coloured and make very popular vivarium pets. Most *Elaphe* species can grow to 6ft.

Aesculapian Snake (Elaphe longissima) This European species is believed to be the one used as a symbol of medicine. It was first chosen by the priests of ancient Greece who worshipped at the temple erected to their god of healing, Asklepos, as being an earthly representative with similar divine powers. The symbol was later taken over by the Romans. So the story goes, a snake was brought back to Rome to alleviate an outbreak of plague, but escaped and swam across to the island in the River Tiber; a hospital now occupies the site where a temple to the Roman god Aesculapius was built. Many of these snakes were liberated at health resorts and baths by the Romans during their occupation of western Europe, so as to spread the healing influence of their god. This could well explain the present, rather scattered distribution of this species, in parts of Switzerland, Germany, France and Spain. It is really a species of south-east Europe and Asia Minor.

The slender body, up to 6ft long, is a uniform yellow-grey to olive-brown. Small white spots form an open meshwork pattern. It frequents woodland, often at high altitude, and is an expert climber. Prey is first constricted. One of the author's specimens lived for eight years.

Leopard Snake (*Elaphe situla*) This exceedingly beautiful colubrid occurs in south and eastern Europe, Asia Minor, also south Italy, Sicily and Malta. The background colour is grey, with a row of brick-red, transverse patches along the back, and further markings along the sides. It usually inhabits dry localities, in scrubland and on mountain slopes.

Two further species which may be encountered in Europe, and which have a preference for dry localities in woodlands, rocky places and vineyards, are sometimes kept. One is the Four-lined Snake (*Elaphe quator-lineata*), which inhabits Italy, Sicily, Yugoslavia, Albania and Greece. The colour is a greenish-brown, with four dark stripes along the body, usually broken up in young individuals. The other is the Ladder Snake ((*E. scalaris*), which occurs in Spain and along the Mediterranean coast of France. Colour is grey to grey-brown. Darker, longitudinal stripes with cross-bars give the impression of a ladder along its body.

Corn Snake (*Elaphe guttata*) This American species, a very handsome one and a vivarium favourite, is coloured a reddish-brown, with a row of large, even redder round patches bordered in black along its back. The belly is chequered in black and white. It ranges through the south and eastern States, in particular the coastal plain and pine barrens of New Jersey, Delaware and Maryland. It is a good climber and a constrictor. It can even grip on to rough bark and climb up a tree-trunk with its ventral scales, without falling off.

Pilot Black Snake or Rat Snake (*Elaphe obsoleta*) This species might be confused with the Black Snake (*Coluber constrictor*). The latter has smooth scales and is black all over; the Pilot Snake has keeled scales along its back, and traces of the juvenile markings. When young it is more greenish, with brown patches. It climbs well and inhabits wooded hilly country over a wide area of the eastern States, including the Appalachian Mountains. The name 'pilot' is based on folklore—that it will lead a rattlesnake away from danger.

Vivaria: as for King snakes (below).

King snakes (*Lampropeltis*)

King snakes are average-sized American colubrids, between 3 and 4ft long. They are attractively marked, and make docile pets. Their sinuous and graceful bodies can cling on to the smallest of projections. There is much variation in colour and markings, even within the same species. King snakes have a peculiar fondness for a diet of other snakes, including even the rattlesnakes, thanks to an apparent immunity from their bite.

American King Snake (*Lampropeltis getulus*) This species is widely distributed over North America; it is divided into a number of sub-species which are given local names. Each has a distinctive colour pattern.

Eastern King Snake (*Lampropeltis getulus getulus*) This is the typical sub-species which occurs in the eastern coastal region. The dark ground-colouring is marked along the back with yellow and white cross-bars. It is frequently seen close to water, in conifer woods and on farmland.

Florida King Snake (*Lampropeltis getulus floridana*)   This is a brown to black sub-species marked with cross-bands in yellow. The black belly is chequered with white and yellow. It frequents more open country on grassland in the Gulf States.

Speckled King Snake (*Lampropeltis getulus holbrooki*)   A dull, greenish background is heavily speckled with small yellow spots. It frequents sandy areas and conifer woods, and occurs in the Mississippi basin. It is a common sight in and around old buildings.

Californian King Snake (*Lampropeltis getulus californiae*)   There are two colour forms of this westerly sub-species. In one the dark-brown background is ringed in creamy yellow. In the other the yellow runs in stripes along the body. This snake inhabits the drier, more desert regions.

Common Milk Snake (*Lampropeltis triangulum triangulum*)   In this sub-species there are large red to brown patches, with smaller ones along the sides, on the paler background. It occurs in Maine, New Hampshire and southwards through the Appalachians to New Jersey and Florida. Here it intergrades with the Coastal Plains Milk Snake (*Lampropeltis triangulum temporalis*). A distinguishing feature is the single row of blotches along the back of the Common Milk Snake, in contrast to the three or five rows of *L. t. temporalis*. There is no truth in the popular belief that these snakes suck milk from cows. More likely they are after the rodents which inhabit farms.

Scarlet Milk Snake (*Lampropeltis doliata annulata*)   This striking sub-species has a succession of rings, coloured red, black and yellow, repeated in succession along its body, thus resembling closely the venomous Coral Snake (*Micrurus*). It is a southerly snake which inhabits wooded country, even entering gardens where it may be discovered hidden under a stone or log. It is only about 12in long. Another, similar looking species, is the Scarlet Snake (*Cnemorpha*), also found in the south. Before handling these brightly coloured snakes it would be wise to consult colour photos to acquaint oneself with the colour patterns, so as to distinguish the harmless species from the true Coral Snake (see Bibliography).

Mole Snake (*Lampropeltis calligaster*)   As its name suggests this species burrows frequently. It is a uniform brown when adult, but marked with numerous, reddish-brown spots in the young stage. It is mostly confined to the south-eastern States.

Vivaria: from the above selection of King snakes the reader should be able to choose an attractive and interesting pet. The vivarium should contain climbing perches, a place to hide under, and the usual dish of drinking-water. The snake can be allowed to hibernate, if so desired. Most of the above species of the genera *Coluber, Elaphe, Lampropeltis* and *Pituophis* (below), will take mice, rats and possibly eggs as a staple diet, to which can be added any wild-caught small mammals.

Ground Constrictors (*Pituophis*)

The Pine Snake (*Pituophis melanoleucus*), and the Bull Snake (*Pituophis catenifer*) are powerful ground snakes which can grow to 6ft or more. Both are constrictors, and will enter burrows in search of prey. They can produce a loud and alarming hiss by forcibly deflating the lungs so that the breath blows across a projection in the epiglottis. Apart from a rather powerful bite, they are harmless. The Pine Snake is coloured grey, with a series of rusty brown patches on its back and sides. It inhabits sandy, mountain areas, and conifer woods in the eastern States. The Bull Snake is much more a yellowish to pale-brown colour and is covered in a series of dark blotches. It belongs to the open prairie of the mid-West.

Vivarium: as for King snakes (immediately above) depending upon size and room required.

African Egg-eating Snake (*Dasypeltis scabra*)

Many snakes feed on birds' eggs, which they swallow and digest, including most of the shell, but in this genus there is a special device for removing and rejecting the shell. The mouth and neck can distend to a remarkable degree in order to accommodate even a hen's egg. Tips of the neck vertebrae project from the wall of the gullet, and these six or eight sharp tips act as a saw to cut through the shell as it passes through. The shell then collapses, and the neck muscles force its contents into the stomach. The shell is ejected.

This harmless snake grows to only 2ft 6in. It has a curious way of warning off an intruder by twisting its body into coils, so that the strongly keeled scales on adjacent coils rub together and produce a loud, rasping noise. It may also strike with open mouth.

This, the common species, is usually a greyish colour, with a series of black blotches down its back, bordered by whitish scales. It is widely distributed from southern Arabia to Africa's Cape Province.

Vivarium: as for King snakes (page 132).

African Mole Snake (Pseudaspis cana)
This widespread snake occurs over most of the African subcontinent south of the Sahara. It can grow up to 6ft and is coloured a glossy, ebony black in most specimens. It is valued on farmland as a hunter of rodents, which far outweighs its occasional lapse as a stealer of chickens and eggs. In areas where plague is endemic it is a valuable ally.

Vivarium: as for King snakes (page 132), with suitable heating.

CHAPTER 8

Crocodiles and Alligators

OF all living animals, this Order, the Loricata or Crocodilia, more than any other, recalls the great Mezozoic Era when reptiles dominated this world. Its members are the nearest modern reptiles to the dinosaurs, and have altered little from their early ancestors. All the living species have a similar build and behaviour. They are well adapted to an aquatic life, but can also emerge on to land, and will spend long periods basking in sunshine. Most of the twenty-five species belong to tropical lands, along rivers, lake borders and in marshes.

The word crocodile is of Latin origin, and was given to the Nile Crocodile by the Romans during their north African occupation. When the Spaniards settled in tropical America they called the large reptiles they noticed *el lagarto*, meaning a lizard. From this we get the word alligator. One external feature which distinguishes crocodiles from alligators is the former's notch on each side of the upper jaw. The fourth lower tooth fits into this and can be seen when the mouth is closed. In alligators this tooth fits into a socket in the upper jaw, and so cannot be seen.

Crocodilians show many features for an aquatic life. The body is streamlined, the toes webbed, and the eyes and nostrils situated on top of the head. The powerful tail is laterally compressed and used for swimming, or for sweeping an unwary victim into the water. Drifting along the surface, with eyes and nostrils just breaking the water, prey is stealthily approached, then caught with a sudden snap. When submerged the nostrils and ears can be closed with flaps. The nose cavity is drawn into a long tube surrounded by bone, and extends far back to where it joins the wind-pipe; a valve can close this so that the mouth can remain open without inhaling water. This enables a crocodile to drown its prey without choking. On land it lies motionless and, in its very simulative camouflage, could be mistaken for a log; so here again an animal can be caught by surprise.

The jaws, once closed, are difficult to open. Food is swallowed whole or, if too large, torn apart with violent shakes of the head. Sometimes it is stored away. During long rest periods the mouth is often opened, which could help in temperature control as the moisture inside the mouth evaporates and cools. During mating, which usually takes place in water, there is much roaring and fighting among the males. Eggs are laid in heaped-up piles of rotting vegetation, or in warm sand. The female will guard her clutch, and uncover them when she hears the calling of the babies just about to hatch.

Family Crocodilidae

Salt-water or Estuarine Crocodile (Crocodylus porosus)
This is the largest living reptile, and one of the most dangerous crocodiles. Even young specimens can be aggressive. It lives in the river mouths and coastal swamps along the Bay of Bengal, across the Malayan coast to the Solomons, New Guinea, northern Australia and the Barrier Reef. It has been known to reach 30ft. Even after five years the author's young specimen was still inclined to bite.

Nile Crocodile (Crocodylus niloticus)
This species, well known to the ancients, extends throughout the major part of Africa wherever there are rivers or marshes and lakes. Specimens up to 20ft are known. However, as with other species, it is much in need of protection, because of hunters who are after short-term profits in selling skins for the leather trade. In places it is now almost extinct, in others it has been reintroduced.

Marsh Crocodile or Mugger (Crocodylus palustris)
This is an Indian and Singalese species, with a broader and shorter snout than the others. A good size is 12ft. It does not appear to attack man.

135

Family Gavialidae

Gharial (Gavialis gangeticus)
This north Indian species has a long, slender snout, which can be swept through the water at speed in order to catch fish on which it mainly subsists. It grows to 20ft. A smaller species with similar snout is the False Gharial (*Tomistoma schlegeli*) of Borneo. Both are said to be harmless to man.

Family Alligatoridae

Broad-nosed and Black Caimans
Caimans or Jacares are crocodilians of Central and South America. In addition to bony scutes embedded in the back, they have them under the belly scales. This could help to protect them from injury when thrown against rocks in a swift-flowing stream. The Broad-nosed species (*Caiman latirostris*), occurs in the rivers of Paraguay and Brazil. It owes its other name of Spectacled Caiman to the bony ridge between the eye sockets, which resembles the nose bow of a pair of spectacles. It grows to about 6ft. A much larger species, the Black Caiman (*Melanosuchus niger*) ranges beyond the Amazon into what was formerly the Guianas and the Orinoco basin. Large numbers are hunted every year in the Amazon. Small specimens of both species are commonly sold as pets.

Mississippi Alligator (Alligator mississipiensis)
This is one of the more northerly species of crocodilian, and today is mainly concentrated in the swamps and lakes of the southern states of the USA, especially in the Everglades of Florida. It has a broad, rounded snout, and is more darkly coloured than the true crocodiles. Young specimens are much paler, with yellow markings on the flanks. This alligator usually hibernates in holes dug into a muddy bank. Because of extensive hunting it is now given protection, and most of the skins are obtained from alligator farms. George, the London Zoo alligator, lived for about forty years and had, by then, lost most of its teeth.
Vivaria: 7. In the vivarium hobby small specimens are usually

kept, and normally give little trouble until they outgrow their home, when they may have to be presented to the local zoo. They can be fed on raw meat and fish, frogs and other aquatic animals. Study of stomach contents has revealed that small crocodilians will eat insects and other small invertebrates.

CHAPTER 9

Tortoises and Terrapins

THESE truly remarkable reptiles of the Order Chelonia or Testudines, have the distinction of being among the most ancient of reptiles, and are known to have existed well before the appearance of dinosaurs, some 200 million years ago. The reason for this ancient lineage is probably their unique build—a kind of mobile fortress made up of a bony shell which encloses the entire animal. This is fused to the rib-cage and backbone; the limb girdles which connect the legs are inside. The shell is covered with a pattern of horny scales, called shields, and consists of an upper half, the carapace, and a lower half, the plastron. Colour and shell arrangement are useful in identification. Since the rib-cage is immovable, breathing is carried out by a pumping action of the neck, aided by muscle contractions at the back of the throat. If the head is moved sharply this causes a hissing or throaty sound, the only noise made by chelonians. The horny beak has no teeth.

All species, including turtles which are sea-going, lay eggs on land in decaying vegetation, the soil or in sand, and leave them to incubate and hatch independently. During mating some form of courtship may take place. A useful guide to sex, apart from the brighter colouring of some males, is the male's thicker tail in which the cloacal opening is placed further away from the shell, also the hollow in the plastron.

The senses of chelonians are moderate. They can see and hear, also smell, and appear to have a colour discrimination. Most reponses are due to earth and water vibrations.

Size varies from small terrapins to the Giant Tortoises on the Galapagos islands in the Pacific and on the Aldabras in the Indian Ocean. Some of these are among the oldest living animals, having reached ages of up to 150 years or more. Estimates of age by counting the rings on the shields cannot be relied on.

The order consists of some 225 species. Whereas, in some countries, like America, it is customary to refer to all chelonians as turtles (ie landturtle, pondturtle and seaturtle), in Britain, one speaks of land-forms as tortoises, freshwater species as pond tortoises or terrapins, and those in the sea as turtles.

Family Testudinidae—Land Tortoises

Members of this family have domed shells without hinges, stumpy and elephantine legs with blunt claws, no toe webs, and normally do not swim. They are mostly vegetarian, and include the Giant Tortoises as well as the Mediterranean species kept as pets in Britain and Europe.

Mediterranean species

These belong to the largest genus of tortoises and include those usually kept as pets. Most commonly imported of all, for the pet trade, is the Spur-thighed or Mediterranean Tortoise (*Testudo graeca*). Its main range is along the north African coast, but it is found from Morocco eastwards as far as Iran, and also in southern Spain. An adult is 8–12in long; it can be identified by the undivided shield (supra-caudal) above the tail, and conical tubercles behind each hind-leg. Colour is yellow and black. The shields of the carapace are yellow, edged in black, with dots in the middle. The yellow plastron has large, triangular black patches. It inhabits scrubland and semi-desert, among sand and rocks. The scientific epithet, *graeca*, could be more properly applied to the next two species.

This pet tortoise can live up to a hundred years. The famous tortoise, Timothy, kept by Gilbert White's family, lived for fifty-four years.

Hermann's Tortoise (*Testudo hermanni*)   This species occurs in the Balkans, parts of Italy and southern France, also some of the Mediterranean islands. It lives in sandy areas among rocks and woodlands, also in mountains. There are no thigh tubercles, but instead a pointed, horny spur at the end of the tail, larger in the male. The supra-caudal is divided. The carapace is

139

usually yellow, sometimes brightly so, each shield bordered in black with a central patch.

Marginated Tortoise (*Testudo marginata*) This species can be distinguished from other Mediterranean tortoises by the absence of a spur on the tail, or tubercles on the thighs. In adults the rear marginal shields curve outwards, giving the border a more wavy outline. Colour is yellow and black, the shields having black borders. It occurs in southern Greece, in rocky terrain, including mountains.

Horsfield's Tortoise (*Testudo horsfieldii*) This differs from the other species in having only four claws on each limb (normally there are five on each front limb). Colour is brown to olive, either plain or speckled with black. The plastron is rather flat. Range extends from the Caspian to north-west India.

Vivaria: 11. Taken collectively these Mediterranean tortoises all require similar treatment. During warm spells they should be exposed to sunlight outdoors. In the author's experience hibernation is advised. Frost should be guarded against at all times. It is true that some specimens will survive the winter months outdoors, provided that they are in good health and well fed, as in the case of Gilbert White's tortoise. There was a time when, out of a quarter of a million tortoises imported into Britain in one year, it was estimated that over 90 per cent had died by the following year, largely due to neglect. These tortoises can eat a surprising amount of food, and will take a variety of green-stuff, fruit, occasional meat, and may take an interest in bones and chalk. This could help in maintaining their calcium requirements.

Desert Tortoises

The *Gopherus* species are the only members of the family *Testudinidae* represented in America. Habitat is mostly desert surroundings, though they are found in dry and stony country, open woodland, chaparral, sand dunes or coniferous woodland.

Desert Tortoise or Gopher (*Gopherus agassizii*) This semi-desert species occurs in parts of Nevada, Utah, California, and Arizona southward into Mexico. The shell is somewhat oblong, with fairly straight sides. The carapace has a wavy border, and the growth furrows on the shields are well marked. Colour is brown, with yellow centres to the shields. The plastron has a projection in front and rear, and is sometimes made use of to advantage when two males are disputing territory or possession of a female. Adult size is up to some 12in.

There are two further American species. The gopher *G. polyphemus*, occurs in the sandhills and high pinewoods of the coastal regions of the Mexican Gulf, and in the Florida peninsula. Berlandier's Tortoise (*G. berlandieri*), is found in semi-desert country, chaparral, and mesquite and open woods, in southern Texas and north-eastern Mexico.

Vivarium: 11. These desert tortoises require an enclosure well filled with sand and rockwork, and the usual summer-house in which to retire. Like the Mediterranean species they are collected extensively for the pet trade. In nature they feed on grass and desert plants, such as cacti, and their flowers and fruits. Records of longevity in captivity seem to be low, at most three to four years, and may be due to the same reason, ie improper care and neglect.

Tropical Tortoises

There are a few tropical tortoises which attract the interest of pet-keepers, and which have finely marked shells. These will need constant warmth, since they do not normally hibernate.

Leopard Tortoise (Geochelone parfalis) This attractive African species occurs over most of the continent, south of the Equator. It grows to about 30in. The smooth and high, domed shell has a serrated border, especially towards the rear; its colour is pale brown, liberally spotted with dark brown.

Geometric Tortoise (Psammobates geometrica) In this species the dorsal shields are raised into conical humps, from which radiate bright yellow streaks, alternating with black. It lives in the more arid areas of southern Africa. Large numbers are caught for the pet and tourist trade.

Starred Tortoise (Testudo elegans) This highly attractive Indian tortoise has a striking pattern of radiating black stripes on each of the yellow dorsal shields, more so than in the Geometric Tortoise. It is much sought after as a pet. Here again, there is a heavy demand from the pet trade.

South American Tortoise (Testudo denticulata) This is a South American species inhabiting the drier areas. It has a brownish carapace, with paler brown centres in the upper shields. These are heavily marked by the growth rings.

Hinged Tortoise (Kinixys belliana) This member of an African genus parallels the American box turtles (*Terrapene*) in having a hinge which closes the rear carapace on the plastron. The carapace is somewhat flattened and covered with smooth brownish shields which have clearly defined borders and growth rings. This particular species is found in tropical Africa (Botswana, the Transvaal and Zululand).

Vivaria: as for Mediterranean species, but guard against damp and cold.

Family Emydidae—Freshwater Tortoises or Terrapins
Of the various families of freshwater Chelonians this family is the best known, and includes many species kept as pets, especially those which are native to North America. They have various common names, and some are known in the States as sliders or cooters. The word terrapin is derived from an Algonquin Indian word meaning 'water tortoise'.

These species differ from the land tortoises (*Testudo*) in having more streamlined and flatter shells. They also have webbed feet with sharp claws. They are mostly carnivorous, catching most of their prey in water, where also they mate. Eggs are laid on land, in a hole dug by the female. The shell is comparatively smooth, and in some species brightly coloured, especially in the young. Much time is spent at the waterside, basking in the sunshine.

Genus Emys
The genus *Emys* has two species, one European and the other American, both of which are often kept as hardy pets.

European Pond Tortoise (Emys orbicularis) This species is well adapted to the British climate, and indeed was once endemic before the onset of the Ice Age. Formerly it extended as far north as Scandinavia. Today it is confined to the marshes, lakes and canals of central and southern Europe, north-west Africa and western Asia. Germany is the northernmost limit.

The smooth plastron is hinged across the middle, and is a deep olive-brown to reddish-brown, with spots and streaks of yellow. The head, limbs and tail are black, spotted on the head. A large adult can measure up to 14in. A specimen has been kept for 120 years. The author's two males have lived in a water trough in the unheated greenhouse for twenty-six years, and are still in good health.

Vivarium: 10, 13. Sunshine is beneficial, and hibernation is advised. Young specimens are best kept indoors during winter, and fed throughout.

Blanding's Terrapin (Emys blandingi) This species is found in the north-eastern USA, from New York State inland to Illinois, and also around the Great Lakes. It grows to about 8in. Colour of the plastron is yellowish, with large symmetrically arranged dark blotches. Some specimens are very dark and covered with small yellow spots. Head and limbs are also spotted, and the throat is bright yellow. It is somewhat inclined to spend much time on land, but is well adapted to water. A specimen in the Philadelphia Zoological Gardens lived for ten years.

Genus Clemmys

This genus is somewhat similar to *Emys* but has a fixed plastron. Species occur in Africa, Europe, America and Asia. The Caspian terrapin (*Clemmys caspica*) is found in Asia Minor, the Greek islands, Cyprus, the Balkans and Yugoslavia. The flattened carapace widens towards the rear to form an egg-shaped ellipse. It is coloured olive-green, covered in a network of pale yellow lines. The Spanish terrapin, formerly called *C. leprosa*, is now considered a sub-species, *C. caspica leprosa*. It is more yellow-brown, and has orange or yellow stripes on the neck and limbs. It lives in north-west Africa and the Iberian peninsula. There are three species in North America.

Spotted Turtle (Clemmys guttata) This easily recognised

species, one of three in North America, has a smooth, low, black-coloured carapace, each shield containing a clear and sharply defined yellow or orange spot. There are also spots on the head and neck. It occurs in the eastern United States, and along the coastal plain as far as Florida. It is a smallish species, seldom growing to more than 4in, and is more inclined to be aquatic, and inhabit muddy pools and brooks.

Wood Turtle (*Clemmys insculpta*) In contrast to the Spotted Turtles this terrapin has a rough and keeled carapace. Colour is brownish, with a dark head and conspicuous orange throat. It is of moderate size, growing to about 6in. The range overlaps that of *C. guttata* but does not reach the Atlantic coastal plains. Much time is spent on land, wandering about the woods and meadows during the warm season, and visiting water to hibernate. It is a very adaptable, tolerant species, and makes an appealing pet. It has catholic tastes and will eat a variety of food, both plant and animal. Has been kept in the Philadelphia Zoo for twelve years.

Pacific Pond Turtle (*Clemmys marmorata*) This third species of *Clemmys* occurs on the far, Pacific side of North America, and extends from British Columbia to California. The carapace is smooth, short and broad, usually dark, and may be spotted. Due to heavy collecting it is now rare in populated areas.

Genera Chrysemys, Pseudemys and Graptemys

The species within these genera, commonly known as sliders, are by far the most common of the terrapins which are kept as pets. They are mainly American, and are often available in pet shops.

Painted Turtle (*Chrysemys p. picta*) This sub-species, which is the one most frequently sold, occurs in the east, from Nova Scotia and Quebec, southwards to northern Florida. The carapace is low, broad and smooth. Adult size reaches some $4\frac{1}{2}$in. Colour is olive to dark-brown, the marginal shields conspicuously marked with red bands and crescents. The plastron is plain yellow. The head is striped with pale lines, and the dark legs are streaked with red. This is a terrapin of quiet waterways, ponds, ditches and slow streams. It keeps close to water and basks for long intervals.

144

It has been kept for ten years. Painting the shell has nothing to do with its name, and is a habit to be discouraged.

The large genus *Pseudemys* is distributed over much of the States, from New England, south as far as Brazil, also the West Indies. Owing to a great variation in colour and markings, some confusion still exists over exact identification. For further information, the Bibliography should be consulted. Unlike *Chrysemys* the carapace has longitudinal wrinkles, and usually a low ridge down the centre. The genus includes some very attractively coloured species, especially when young, and is divided into three: *scripta*, *rubiventris* and *floridana*.

Among the *Pseudemys scripta*, there is much variation in colour and markings. Even sexes differ, and male specimens tend to turn black, or become melanic, with age. Of the five sub-species the following two are usually available to pet-keepers.

Yellow-bellied Turtle or Slider (*Pseudemys scripta scripta*) This sub-species is confined to the eastern coastal states. Distinctive features are the large yellow crescent behind each eye, and the dark patches on the yellow plastron. The shell is shorter and broader than in other sub-species, and measures about 7in in the adult.

Elegant or Red-eared Turtle (*Pseudemys scripta elegans*) This sub-species, the most widely kept and offered in pet shops, occurs in the states lying between the Great Lakes and the Gulf of Mexico, also from Texas eastwards to Ohio and Louisiana. It has a low greenish carapace minus a ridge, and a bright red patch behind each eye, in place of the yellow crescent of *P. s. scripta*. The plastron is more heavily marked in black. Average adult size is 7in.

Red-bellied Turtle or Cooter (*Pseudemys rubiventris rubra*) The *rubiventris* species is named after its colour—a red or orange plastron. The carapace is somewhat wrinkled lengthwise, but has no ridge. Colour is brownish, covered in a fine net-work pattern. This sub-species is confined to the coastal plains of New York to central Virginia. Demands for the pet trade have made great inroads into populations, and it now appears to be absent from New York.

Coastal Plains Turtle (*Pseudemys floridana floridana*) The widespread *floridana* species extends along the Atlantic coast, through the Gulf States across to Texas. There are some nine sub-species. This one occurs along the coastal plains, from Virginia to Florida. The carapace is dark-brown, with a network of paler lines or rings. The plastron is pale yellow. *Floridana* species are somewhat larger than the other two. One feature is the absence of any notch in the jaw which is more upwardly curved.

Common Map Turtle (*Graptemys geographica*) Members of this genus can be recognised by the tooth-like border to the carapace, which is more accentuated towards the rear. This species is so-called after the contour-like pattern of lines on its head and limbs. The carapace is smooth and has a low, more toothed ridge. The head is large, especially in the female. Colour is an olive-brown. It is very aquatic and stays close to water. Range is through the mid-eastern and mid-western States.

Sawback Turtle (*Graptemys pseudographica*) A distinct feature of this species is the high and toothed keel on the carapace, and a smaller head than *G. geographica*. Among the various pale lines on the head is a prominent, curved stripe in the neck region. It is inclined to eat more water plants than other terrapins do.

Vivaria: 7, 10. Taking all the forgoing *Emydidae* terrapins in general, they require broadly similar care and feeding, with water in which to swim, and a place in the sun out on land. Adult specimens usually give little trouble as pets, provided that they are well fed on a proper diet (see page 53). In some ways it is unfortunate that so many baby terrapins are caught and offered for sale, since so many soon die; their attractive colouring and popularity so often lead them into the hands of an inexperienced owner. This remark is not intended to discourage the reader, but to point out that a high mortality is a well-known fact among conservationists, some of whom would wish that this trade in baby terrapins, as well as that in tortoises, were banned altogether.

Box Turtles—Genus Terrapene

The *Terrapene* species are of especial interest to herpetologists. Although placed scientifically in the same family Emydidae as the above species, its members bear more resemblance to the land tortoises (*Testudinidae*). Like them, a box turtle has a high, domed shell and is well adapted to a terrestrial life. The more terrapin-like features are its ability to enter water (where it may even hibernate) and its fondness for animal prey, as well as plants. A hinge across the centre of the plastron enables it to close the shell entirely. The toes are slightly webbed. Box turtles inhabit the eastern states from New England to Florida, also Texas and Mexico.

Common Box Turtle (*Terrapene carolina carolina*) Of the four sub-species, this typical form is found in the eastern States. Other sub-species are found further inland, and in the Gulf States. The domed carapace is slightly keeled, coloured a horn-brown marked with darker blotches. The tip of the jaw is hooked. The eyes of the male are bright red, in the female they are browner. This terrestrial terrapin inhabits open woodland in the vicinity of water, and roams widely, especially during rainy spells. It will burrow during drought. Feeding is omnivorous, and includes a variety of plants, leaves, grass, fruit and fungi. Adult size is about 6in.

Ornate Box Turtle (*Terrapene ornata*) This attractively marked species is a little smaller than its relative, and grows to about 5½in. The chocolate to reddish-brown, unkeeled carapace is marked with pale radiating lines. Head and limbs are spotted yellow. It occurs through the central States, mostly in prairie country, also in woodland, among sandhills and in swamps, sometimes at high altitudes. It seldom enters water and is usually an inhabitant of semi-arid country. It will burrow during drought or frost. Food is varied, from insects and other small invertebrates to all kinds of plants.

Vivaria: 11, as for the Mediterranean tortoises. A summer-house packed closely with dried leaves makes a suitable retreat. Hibernate in a similar manner. These box turtles can live to a ripe old age, for as long as a hundred years.

Family Kinosternidae—Musk and Mud Turtles

These small-sized terrapins have two closely related genera in America, the Musk turtles (*Sternotherus*) and the Mud turtles (*Kinosternon*). They are somewhat nondescript and dully coloured, and tend to lurk in shallow, muddy water in ponds, ditches, swamps and coastal marshes.

Common Musk Turtle (*Sternotherus odoratus*)

This is one of the commoner species which extends right across the eastern half of the USA. It has a poorly developed plastron leaving wide gaps so that the entire limbs are fully exposed. It is coloured a dull brown, but has a pale stripe along each side of the head and neck. The nose is somewhat pointed. It is small in size, up to 4in. Known locally as the 'Stinkpot' it has glands in between the carapace and plastron which secrete a musky odour. It has been kept for twenty-three years.

Mud Turtle (*Kinosternon subrubrum*)

Of the three American species this is the best known, and occurs in the eastern and Gulf States, extending northwards to the Great Lakes. It is of similar size and appearance to the Musk turtle. The plastron is better hinged to cover the limbs, however, and the head and neck stripe is missing.

Vivarium: 7, 10. Provide ample mud in shallow water. These terrapins will feed on fish, snails and other water creatures, insects, and are determined scavengers.

Family Trionychidae—Soft-shelled Turtles

This peculiar family has special features for an aquatic life. The flattened shell is only partly ossified, and is covered with an undivided, leathery skin. This enables the terrapin to burrow into the bottom, and to squeeze in between underwater rocks and stones. Limbs are broadly webbed and three-toed (hence the family name). The nostrils are placed at the end of a tubular snout. These terrapins occur in North America, Asia and Africa. They feed on small water animals and, because they are inclined to bite, need careful handling.

Soft-shelled Turtle (*Amyda ferox ferox*)

This is a member of a widespread genus extending over much of the USA, apart from the western half and the eastern coastal states. This particular and typical sub-species is found in Florida, and is common in the Everglades. It is the largest of the 'soft-shells', reaching a length of 18in. Colour is a greyish-brown on the carapace, marked with darker blotches. The plastron is white. It is almost entirely aquatic, and will lie for hours in shallow water, its snout just protruding above the surface. By gulping water in and out of the mouth it can 'breathe' by absorbing dissolved oxygen through the lining of its throat. Almost any kind of small water creature is caught by stealth.

Vivarium: 7, 10. Soft-shelled terrapins obviously need plenty of water-space, in a fairly roomy aquarium, or an outdoor pool in summer, which contains a good supply of mud or loose sand. The water should be shallow so that the head can be held above it.

Family Chelidae—Snake-necked Terrapins

This is a family of side-necked Chelonians, mostly South American, in which the neck is twisted sideways when retracted. They also occur in South Africa, Australia and New Guinea.

Snake-necked Terrapin (*Chelodina longicollis*)

This extraordinary species inhabits Australia, and is usually kept more as a curiosity. It has an exceptionally long neck, and bright yellow eyes. When retracted the neck is twisted sideways into the neck-folds.

By resting on the bottom, it can extend its neck in periscope fashion so that its head is just above water. It is rather small, up to about 4½in long, and quite inoffensive. It feeds on small fish which are caught with a darting movement of the neck.

Vivarium: 7, 10, or an aquarium with a muddy bottom. This species is mainly aquatic.

Family Pelomedusidae—Side-necked Terrapins

Cape Terrapin (*Pelomedusa subrufra*)

This is a well-known South African representative of the

Pelomedusidae family. It occurs in swamps, pools and lakes in the veldt country south of the Sahara, and measures up to about 12in. The smooth and dark shell is very flattened. It can emit an unpleasant smell from the glands, but even so is eaten by the natives. The dry season is spent buried in the mud.

Vivarium: as for the Mud Turtle (page 148).

Some Useful Tips to Remember

1 Because of their sensitive skins, amphibians should be handled as little as possible.

2 Before adding a fresh specimen to the collection, keep it in quarantine for a few days, so as to avoid possible infection.

3 One's nose is the best guide to any sign of pollution.

4 Snakes are Houdinis at escaping through the smallest apertures. Make sure that all movable parts and joints of their container are firmly fixed, especially doors.

5 Some people are genuinely terrified of reptiles, especially snakes. Always give warning before showing one.

6 Snakes do not attack, but only bite in self defence. Never trust a venomous snake—it should always be treated with caution.

7 'Variety is the spice of life' applies to amphibians and reptiles as much as it does to us, where food is concerned.

8 Don't handle a lizard by its tail—it may come off.

9 Do not subject an amphibian or reptile to sudden changes in temperature. Never disturb one in hibernation.

10 Difficult feeders should be given a choice of all kinds of food, so that they can select which they prefer; the animal knows best. This is common practice in zoos.

11 Amphibians and reptiles which normally hibernate will not do so in warm surroundings. Place in a cold but frost-free retreat, such as a shed, unheated garage or cellar.

12 Because normal glass filters out the valuable ultra-violet rays, direct sunlight should be provided as often as possible for those reptiles which normally bask. The U-V lamp is a valuable asset in vivarium keeping.

APPENDIX 2

Plants Suitable for the Aquarium, Viviarium, Pond and Reptiliary

THE use of land-plants in any of the above situations is partly for show, but also for cover, since they give the shade and damp corners necessary for some occupants. Aquatic plants provide similar cover, as well as a medium for spawning, they also act as oxygenators. Some animals may eat the plants, which will then require screening if they are needed only for decoration.

For the Cold-water Aquarium
As spawning media and for shelter:
Canadian Pondweed (*Elodea canadensis*). A prolific grower and
    oxygenator.
Water Milfoil (*Myriophyllum spicatum*).
Hornwort (*Ceratophyllum demersum*).
Water Starwort (*Callitriche palustris*).
Willow-moss (*Fontinalis antipyretica*). An aquatic moss.
Water Crowfoot (*Ranunculus aquatilis*).
Italian Tape-grass (*Vallisneria spiralis*). Naturalised in parts of
    Britain, near warm water outflows.
Eagria densa and *Lagarosiphon major*. Both are related to
    Elodea, but have no English common names.
The last three are available from aquarium dealers.

Floating plants for cover:
Duckweed (*Lemna* sp). Various species are available.
Ivy Duckweed (*Lemna trisulca*).
Crystalwort (*Riccia fluitans*). An aquatic liverwort.
Water Fern (*Azolla filiculoides*). Locally naturalised in Britain
    (America).

K   153

Water Fern (*Salvinia braziliensis*). Normally used in tropical tanks, but grows well during summer in cooler water.

Frog-bit (*Hydrochaerus morsus-ranae*).

For the Tropical Aquarium
Since the hobby of tropical fish-keeping has a wide following, and there are plenty of books on the subject and aquarium dealers competent to advise on appropriate plants, no list is given here.

For the Pond
Any of the above native water-plants, also:

Waterlilies. The native White Waterlily (*Nymphaea alba*) and the Yellow Waterlily or Brandy-bottle (*Nuphar lutea*) are a little too large and robust for the average garden pond. However, there are many smaller forms available from dealers:

Pondweed (*Potamogeton* sp). Various species are available.

Arrowhead (*Saggittaria natans*).

Water Violet (*Hottonia palustris*).

Water Soldier (*Stratiotes aloides*).

Marsh and border plants:

Yellow Flag (*Iris pseudacorus*). A prolific grower which needs control. A number of smaller species are available from dealers.

Reed Mace (*Typha latifolia*).

Bur-reed (*Sparganum erectum*).

Sweet Flag (*Acorus calamus*).

Horse-tail (*Equisetum*—various species).

Bogbean (*Menyanthes trifoliata*).

Kingcup (*Caltha palustris*).

For the Vivarium
Most of the following plants are available from nurseries or florists, and are usually sold as house plants. Since this is a popular hobby, there are many books on the subject, and so the following is a limited list.

In warm, shady surroundings:

Maidenhair (*Adiantum*—various species). The British species is now rare and best avoided.

Parlour Palm (*Aspidistra lurida* and *A. elatior*).

Rubber Plant (*Crassula* sp). Various species are available.

Arrow-root (*Maranta leuconeura*).

Vine (*Philodendron scandens*). A useful climber.

Fig (*Ficus* sp). Various species are available.

Wandering Jew (*Tradescantia albovitatta*).

In warm, bright surroundings:

Balsam or Busy Lizzy (*Impatiens holstii*).

Cape Geranium (*Pelargonium* sp). Various species are available.

Cheese Plant (*Monstera deliciosa*).

Wandering Jew (*T. albovitatta*).

In cool, dampish surroundings:

Aralia (*Fatsia japonica*).

Ivies (*Hedera* sp). Various species are available.

Kangaroo Vine (*Cissus antarctica*). A useful climber.

Monstera species.

Fatshedera. This cross between *Fatsia japonica* and *Hedera helix* is a useful climber.

In dry, warm surroundings:

Various cacti, sedums (stonecrops), heaths (*Erica*) and succulents, Christmas Cactus (*Zygocactus*).

For the Reptiliary

Plants will probably be chosen here for attractiveness and design features, but should also be useful for cover. If a rock garden is built on the reptiliary island, or as a pond-surround, plenty of suitable plants should be obtainable from stockists. Rock-gardening is a hobby in its own right, and plenty of relevant books are available.

APPENDIX 3

Societies and Organisations

In Britain:
THE BRITISH HERPETOLOGICAL SOCIETY
Hon Secretary,
British Herpetological Society,
Zoological Society of London,
London NW1
The British Herpetological Society publishes a journal and a newsletter.

In the United States:
THE AMERICAN SOCIETY OF ICHTHYOLOGISTS AND
HERPETOLOGISTS
Secretary (Bruce Collette),
Bureau of Commercial Fisheries,
US National Museum,
Washington DC 20560.

THE HERPETOLOGISTS LEAGUE
Secretary and Treasurer (J. Whitfield Gibbons),
Savannah River Ecology Labs,
PO Drawer E,
Aiken, S. Carolina 29801.
The American Society of Ichthyologists and Herpetologists publishes the journal, *Copeia,* and the Herpetologists League publishes *Herpetologica.*

Bibliography

BRITISH SPECIES

Knight, Maxwell. *Frogs, Toads and Newts in Britain*. Leicester: Brockhampton Press, 1963
——. *Reptiles in Britain*. Leicester: Brockhampton Press, 1965
Smith, Malcolm. *British Amphibians and Reptiles*. London: Collins, New Naturalist, 1951

REGIONAL

Bishop, Sherman C. *Handbook of Salamanders*. New York: Comstock, and London: Constable, 1943
Carr, Archie. *Handbook of Turtles*. New York: Comstock, and London: Constable, 1952
Conant, Roger. *Reptiles and Amphibians of the Northeastern States*. Philadelphia, Pa: Philadelphia Zoological Society, 1947
Hellmich, Walter. *Reptiles and Amphibians of Europe*. trs Alfred Leutscher. London: Blandford Press, 1962
Isemonger, R. M. *Snakes of Africa*. London: Nelson, 1962
Pope, Clifford. *Snakes of North-eastern USA*. New York: New York Zoological Society, 1946
Rose, Walter. *Reptiles and Amphibians of Southern Africa*. Cape Town: Maskew Miller, 1950
Smith, Hobart M. *Handbook of Lizards*. New York: Comstock, and London: Constable, 1946
Steward, J. E. *Tailed Amphibians of Europe*. Newton Abbot: David & Charles, 1969
Truitt, J. O. *A Guide to the Snakes of Florida*. Miami Fla: Miami Museum of Science and Natural History, 1960

157

GENERAL AND BIOLOGICAL

Bellairs, Angus. *Reptiles*. London: Hutchinson, University Library, 1957

Bellairs, Angus, and Carrington, Richard. *World of Reptiles*. London: Chatto & Windus, 1966

Leutscher, Alfred. *Study of Reptiles and Amphibians*. London: Blandford Press, 1963

Noble, Kingsley G. *Biology of the Amphibia*. New York: McGraw-Hill, 1931; repr Dover Publications, 1954

Parker, H. W. *Snakes*. London: Robert Hale, 1963

———. *Snakes*. London: British Museum (Natural History), 1965

Vogel, Zdenek. *Reptiles and Amphibians*. London: Paul Hamlyn, 1966

PET-KEEPING

Allen, E. Ross, and Neill, W. T. *Keep Them Alive*. Silver Springs, Fla: Ross Allen Reptile Institute, 1954

Hoke, John. *Turtles and Their Care*. New York: Franklin Watts, 1963

———. *Terrariums*. New York: Franklin Watts, 1972

Knight, Maxwell. *Tortoises and How to Keep Them*. Leicester: Brockhampton Press, 1964

Latimer-Sayer, D. *Indoor Aquaria*. London: English Universities Press, 1967

Leutscher, Alfred. *The Tortoise as a Pet*. London: Universities Federation for Animal Welfare pamphlet, 1960

Noel-Hume, Ivor and Audrey. *Tortoises, Terrapins and Turtles*. London: Frederick Muller, 1954

Wright, W. J. *Care of the Common Pet Tortoise*. Published privately, Porthleven, Cornwall

———. *Care of Terrapins*. Published privately, Porthleven, Cornwall

BOOKS IN COLOUR

Cochran, Doris. *Living Amphibians of the World*. London: Hamish Hamilton, 1960

Schmidt, Karl, and Inger, Robert. *Living Reptiles of the World*. London: Hamish Hamilton, 1957

Index

Numbers in italic refer to illustrations

Index of Latin Names